WHAT YOUR COLLEAGUES ARE SAYING...

"This book reimagines the professional learning community as a dynamic space where educators leverage their collective expertise to brainstorm possibilities and generate innovative ideas. This book is grounded in the belief that educators are professionals in their field and empowers them to transform insights into actionable initiatives that drive meaningful change."

—**Sarah D. Ortega**, Instructional Coach,
Chula Vista Elementary School District

"PLC+ is a game changer for professional learning communities. Fisher and Frey provide a research-driven, equity-centered framework that empowers educators to collaborate with clarity and purpose. This book is an essential guide for teams looking to enhance student learning through collective efficacy and actionable strategies."

—**Aida Allen-Rotell**, Learning Technician and Co-Author of
PLC+: A Playbook for Instructional Leaders

"*Your Introduction to PLC+: Building Collaborative Teams That Drive Student Success* by Doug Fisher and Nancy Frey is a fantastic resource that enhances the work around teacher collective efficacy by providing collaborative structures to improve student learning. It also strengthens teacher and leader capacity through reflective practices and data-driven decision-making, making it an essential guide for professional learning communities at any level."

—**Kim West**, Corwin Faculty Member, former Kramer IB World
School Coordinator and Math Instructional Coach, Dallas ISD

"Finally, a PLC book that doesn't just rehash old ideas but actually makes them better. *Your Introduction to PLC+* bridges research and reality, delivering actionable strategies with an unwavering focus on equity. This book empowers teams, drives real impact, and elevates student success."

—**Tyler Gilbert**, Academic Coach, Calwa Elementary School,
Fresno Unified School District

"A must-read for all educators committed to continuous growth, impactful collaboration, and lasting impact in education. This book provides the essential strategies every team needs to collaborate effectively, maximize their impact, and drive meaningful student success."

—**Olivia Amador-Valerio**, Corwin Professional Learning Consultant and Author, Bilingual
Educator, Reading and Language Arts Specialist, Instructional Coach and Leader

"Believing in continuous improvement and improving are two different things. Closing this gap is exactly what this book does for teaching and learning. This groundbreaking resource reimagines how professional learning communities can drive meaningful change in our schools and classrooms. Fisher and Frey have beautifully designed a practical guide that goes beyond theory to deliver actionable strategies for implementation—boosting the collective efficacy of our communities. What sets this work apart is how it centers equity throughout the PLC process, ensuring that all students benefit from our collective efforts. This isn't just another education book to add to your shelf; it's a vital companion that will accelerate the impact by enhancing how your team approaches collaborative work. If you're seeking to build a more responsive, equitable, and effective learning community, Fisher and Frey's work is absolutely essential."

—**John Almarode**, Professor of Education, James Madison University

"This book is a transformative approach to professional learning communities, grounded in liberatory design principles that remove barriers to learning and elevate teacher agency. By centering collaboration, inquiry, and collective responsibility, Fisher and Frey honor the expertise of educators as the key drivers of meaningful change. PLC+ isn't just another framework—it's a movement toward more just, informed, and impactful teaching that empowers both teachers and students to thrive."

—**Kierstan Barbee**, Professional Learning Consultant

"*Your Introduction to PLC+: Building Collaborative Teams That Drive Student Success—An Illustrated Playbook* is a must-have for schools that are seeking to experience immediate transformation of their teacher teams! The content of this playbook is designed to equip educators with the tools to foster growth and achievement for every learner, regardless of background or circumstance! Educators are given the opportunity to know how to measure the impact of their collective collaboration in real time with the multitude of job-embedded experiences and tools that are included throughout this publication. What has always been evident in the PLC+ model within this uniquely designed playbook format is HOW the authors provide teams the knowledge and skills to engage with each other to overcome challenges and produce intended outcomes through a commitment of unified ACTIONS! Another key feature of this book is the use of the *Liberatory Design approach* created by the National Equity Project. This approach is a cornerstone to elevating processes that guide the decision-making techniques of PLC+ teams through a dynamic cycle of improvement efforts that meet the diverse and evolving needs of schools. Since the inception of the PLC+ model six years ago, many educational communities have been transformed throughout the world and are embracing the results of growth in student and educator learning. With confidence, I know that the tools and experiences in this publication are sure to create many more school cultures that generate success for all!"

—**Sonja Hollins-Alexander**, Content Advisor and Scholar

"*Your Introduction to PLC+: Building Collaborative Teams That Drive Student Success* is an essential guide for educators looking to strengthen professional learning communities and improve student outcomes. Using a clear framework and practical strategies, this book empowers teachers and leaders to collaborate effectively to drive meaningful change in their schools. A must-read for anyone committed to fostering a culture of continuous learning and student success!"

—**Toni Faddis**, Former Principal and Corwin Author

YOUR INTRODUCTION TO PLC+

Your Introduction to PLC+

Building Collaborative Teams That Drive Student Success

An Illustrated Playbook with 40+ Videos

DOUGLAS FISHER
NANCY FREY
Illustrations by TARYL HANSEN

CORWIN

CORWIN

FOR INFORMATION:

Corwin

A Sage Company

2455 Teller Road

Thousand Oaks, California 91320

(800) 233-9936

www.corwin.com

Sage Publications Ltd.

1 Oliver's Yard

55 City Road

London EC1Y 1SP

United Kingdom

SAGE Publications India Pvt. Ltd.

Unit No 323-333, Third Floor, F-Block

International Trade Tower Nehru Place

New Delhi 110 019

India

SAGE Publications Asia-Pacific Pte. Ltd.

18 Cross Street #10-10/11/12

China Square Central

Singapore 048423

Vice President and
 Editorial Director: Monica Eckman

Senior Director and Publisher, Content and
 Product: Lisa Luedeke

Content Development Editor: Sarah Ross

Product Associate: Zachary Vann

Production Editor: Nicole Burns-Ascue

Copy Editor: Beth Ginter

Typesetter: C&M Digitals (P) Ltd.

Proofreader: Sarah Duffy

Indexer: Integra

Graphic Designer: Gail Buschman

Marketing Manager: Megan Naidl

Copyright © 2025 by Corwin Press, Inc.

All rights reserved. Except as permitted by U.S. copyright law, no part of this work may be reproduced or distributed in any form or by any means, or stored in a database or retrieval system, without permission in writing from the publisher.

When forms and sample documents appearing in this work are intended for reproduction, they will be marked as such. Reproduction of their use is authorized for educational use by educators, local school sites, and/or noncommercial or nonprofit entities that have purchased the book.

All third-party trademarks referenced or depicted herein are included solely for the purpose of illustration and are the property of their respective owners. Reference to these trademarks in no way indicates any relationship with, or endorsement by, the trademark owner.

ISBN: 978-1-0718-7117-1

Library of Congress Control Number: 2025935540

DISCLAIMER: This book may direct you to access third-party content via web links, QR codes, or other scannable technologies, which are provided for your reference by the author(s). Corwin makes no guarantee that such third-party content will be available for your use and encourages you to review the terms and conditions of such third-party content. Corwin takes no responsibility and assumes no liability for your use of any third-party content, nor does Corwin approve, sponsor, endorse, verify, or certify such third-party content.

CONTENTS

Acknowledgments — ix

Introduction — 1

Module 1: Where Are We Going? — 49

Module 2: Where Are We Now? — 75

Module 3: How Do We Move Learning Forward? — 101

Module 4: What Did We Learn Today? — 131

Module 5: Who Benefited and Who Did Not? — 165

Module 6: PLC+ Planning, Progress Monitoring, and Success Tools — 197

Conclusion — **229**

References — **231**

Index — **237**

Visit the companion website at
https://companion.corwin.com/courses/PLC
for downloadable resources.

ACKNOWLEDGMENTS

PLC+ ADVISORY GROUP

Aida Allen-Rotell, MA
Bilingual Teacher
and Leader,
San Diego, CA

Oscar Corrigan, EdD
Administator,
San Diego, CA

John Almarode, PhD
Professor of Education,
Richmond, VA

Sarah Ortega, EdD
Bilingual Teacher
and Leader,
San Diego, CA

James Marshall, PhD
Professor of
Educational
Leadership,
San Diego, CA

Toni Faddis, EdD
Teacher and Leader,
San Diego, CA

Dominique Smith, EdD
Principal,
San Diego, CA

Nicole Law, PhD
Teacher and Leader,
Indianapolis, IN

Marnitta George, PhD
National Board
Certified Teacher,
San Diego, CA

Sonja Hollins-Alexander, EdD
Teacher and Leader,
Atlanta, GA

Tyler Gilbert, MA
Academic Coach,
Fresno, CA

Kierstan Barbee, EdD
Teacher and Coach,
Dallas, TX

Olivia Amador, EdD
Bilingual Teacher and Leader,
San Diego, CA

Woo Williams-Zou, MA, JD
Senior Equity Leadership Consultant,
National Equity Project
Oakland, CA

Kim West, MA
Teacher,
Dallas, TX

Tom Malarkey, MA
Director,
National Equity Project
Oakland, CA

INTRODUCTION

A professional learning community (PLC) is a structured, collaborative approach to professional learning in which educators come together regularly as a team to discuss and reflect on the evidence they collect from students and about their teaching practices with the goal of improving student outcomes. Unlike traditional, top-down professional development models, PLCs are driven by the teachers, who share a commitment to ongoing learning, mutual accountability, and the belief that every student can succeed. Effective PLCs give teachers the autonomy they desire and the level of professionalism they have earned.

Professional learning communities, which have existed for several decades, were originally designed to combat the teacher isolation that was common in the 1950s and 1960s. The idea was that teachers, working together, could positively impact students' learning; the groups would help ensure that the individuals working so hard to make that impact were connected with like-minded colleagues. This turned out to be a good idea, and today the evidence strongly suggests that professional learning communities can positively impact both teacher practice and student achievement.[1]

But—and this is important—these groups work only when done right. Over the decades, researchers and practitioners have learned more about what it means to implement effective professional learning communities. As the evidence has been assembled, processes, procedures, and protocols have been updated and revised. As needed, older practices were abandoned as newer practices were identified.

Enter PLC+, the next-generation professional learning community model designed to ensure that educators are connected with their peers and are impacting student learning in positive ways. This framework stands on the shoulders of the giants who went before us, yet it also reflects new evidence about learning communities that has been collected over the past decade. This book provides an introduction to PLCs in general and then takes a deep dive into an updated structure and system for ensuring that teacher teams are successful—an approach that we call PLC+.

As a high-level overview, PLC+ is fed by Liberatory Design.[2] Liberatory Design, originally developed by the National Equity Project and the K–12 Lab at the Stanford Design School (d.school), is both a process and a practice to address persistent inequities in complex systems in order to foster transformative change. In the PLC+ process, four crosscutting values serve as a foundation for the work that the PLC+ teams do: equity and fairness, high expectations, individual and collective efficacy, and activation. These values give rise to five guiding questions:

1. Where are we going?
2. Where are we now?
3. How do we move learning forward?
4. What did we learn today?
5. Who benefited and who did not?

Each of these questions also serves as the focus of a module in this book; the final module offers guidelines for how teams can work most effectively.

The questions explored in each of the first five modules inspire actions, and teams use protocols to accomplish their work. In other words, as PLC+ teams work together to seek answers to these questions, they generate a complex web of thinking and actions that improve the experience of schooling. A visual representation of this model is included below.

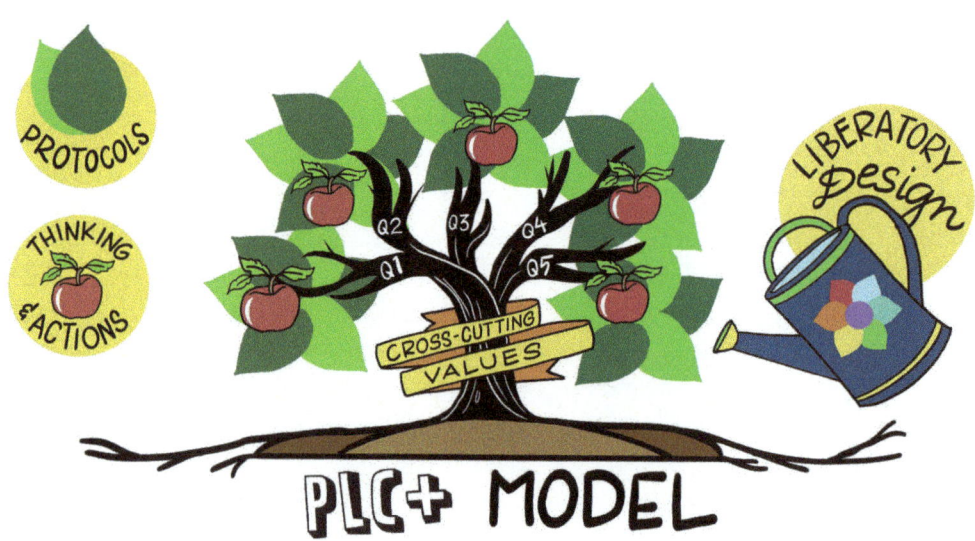

FEATURES OF THIS ILLUSTRATED PLAYBOOK

There are several design features, in addition to the illustrations, that are intended to increase your interaction with the contents. These features are consistent in each of the modules to allow you to develop habits as you interact with the information.

- An **Essential Question** frames each module to help build an organizational framework for processing the information.

- **Two Truths and a Lie** near the beginning of each module allows you to consider several statements and then determine which ones are supported by the research and which one captures a common misconception. We invite you to return to these after reading the module to see if your thinking has been validated or extended.

- **The Story Behind the Question** provides information about why the key question is valuable to teams and the evidence that was used to develop and test it. Understanding the history of PLCs and the continued efforts to improve them, including ideas from the past that have not worked, is important for teams who want to take their work to the next level.

- **Liberatory Design**, an approach to transforming inequity in complex systems, grounds the PLC+ process and helps educators develop authentic and collaborative relationships that support redesigning negative systems, structures, and approaches that are reproducing oppression and contributing to inequitable outcomes and experiences. It builds on systems thinking and design thinking to ensure that discussions and decisions result in improved outcomes for all students.

- **Protocols** are included throughout this book to help teams engage in collaborative conversations. Protocols create structure, facilitate collaboration, and improve communication within teams. Over time, teams can adapt and revise the protocols to fit their specific needs.

Introduction 3

- **Ask a Bot** provides advice on using generative AI as a teaching assistant or thought partner, saving teachers and teams time to focus on the needs of their students. The output from AI should always be reviewed for accuracy and usefulness. Remember, AI systems are biased due to the fact that they scrub content that was created by humans who have implicit biases.

- **Quick Starts** provide opportunities to reflect on the content, prioritize actions, and identify resources you may need. These sections are designed to help you and your team decide which steps can be taken immediately and which ones require additional thought, planning, or time.

- The **Case in Point** in each module offers a scenario and an opportunity to see educators working together to resolve a dilemma. These cases are designed to allow you to practice and apply what you are learning by considering the challenges in the related **What's Your Advice?** feature, which allows you to make recommendations based on what you have learned and experienced. You can also share your advice with your own team members and collectively determine the next steps you believe would appropriately support the people profiled in the case.

- A **Crosscutting Values Check** reminds you of the four values that are integrated into the PLC+ framework: equity and fairness, high expectations, individual and collective efficacy, and activation. In this section, we present some questions aligned with each of the values that encourage reflection and integration into your practices.

- **Self-Assessment** tools allow you to determine the strengths of your team and where you may want to focus additional efforts. Remember, teams are always on a journey, increasing their ability to work together to impact students' learning. As teams become more efficient, the impact that they have on students' learning will increase.

- **Notice and Reflect** appears at the end of every module and invites you to reflect on your learning and take actions of your own: What will you start, stop, and continue? It allows you space to scale your level of understanding so that you can keep learning after finishing the module. It also allows you to interact with colleagues and build your collective efficacy. As we have noted many times: The plus is YOU! You are a valued contributor to your students' learning, your own learning, and your team members' learning.

STRUCTURE OF THIS ILLUSTRATED PLAYBOOK

Following this introduction, we provide an overview module that is intended to build your background knowledge about professional learning communities. We review the history of this idea and its many iterations. In addition, we provide some distinguishing features of the next-generation PLC model: PLC+. Following the introduction, we turn our attention to the PLC+ framework guiding questions:

- **Module 1** focuses on the question *Where are we going?* This module provides information about analyzing standards to identify what students need to learn and be able to do. It includes information about organizing instruction in blocks of standards and how to ensure that students understand their learning journey.

- **Module 2** focuses on the question *Where are we now?* In this module, we argue that teams should pay attention to students' strengths and assets. They should collect evidence from students to identify what they already know so that they can design the learning journey.

- **Module 3** focuses on the question *How do we move learning forward?* This includes attention to instruction, which has been neglected in professional learning community conversations. Further, we note the value of teachers visiting peers' classrooms and talking about the evidence they collect to determine if their instructional moves are making a difference.

- **Module 4** focuses on the question *What did we learn today?* This is the assessment module and includes a number of tools educators can use to determine student progress toward competency. In addition, we focus on the learning of adults and how we can reflect on our efforts to ensure students' learning.

- **Module 5** focuses on the question *Who benefited and who did not?* This requires that we carefully consider the differential impact on students' learning and how we can address those differences. In addition, we note the value of removing barriers to students' learning and identifying needs for supplemental and intensive interventions.

Video 0.1
Introduction from
Doug & Nancy
qrs.ly/hbghoa3

- **Module 6** focuses on the structures and systems required for PLC+ teams to operate effectively and efficiently. Although it comes at the end of the book, as with any playbook, you can decide which move you need when. If your team wants to self-assess their efforts and identify strengths and needs, turning your attention to Module 6 would be wise.

Again, this illustrated playbook is meant to engage *you* and your team. Please mark it up and complete the various tasks. The narrative in each module provides current and tested research as well as informed recommendations for practice for your PLC+. Enjoy!

NOTES

OVERVIEW

WHAT DOES A "PROFESSIONAL LEARNING COMMUNITY" MEAN, ANYWAY?

Teams of educators are powerful. When educators band together, work toward a shared goal, and collect evidence to determine their impact—even when faced with challenges—the results for students are spectacular. In fact, teams of educators are unstoppable whenever they believe they can accomplish each of the following:

- Change the trajectory of students' learning
- Collect and interpret evidence aligned with their goals
- Assume collective responsibility for their own learning and for the learning of their students

In the research world, this is called *collective teacher efficacy*, and it is one of the most powerful things educators can do to accelerate students' learning.[3]

Bandura invented the term *collective efficacy* based on his observation that a group's confidence in its abilities seemed to be associated with greater success.[4] In other words, the assurances people place on their team affects the team's overall performance. In Bandura's words, "Perceived collective efficacy will influence what people choose to do as a group, how much effort they put into it, and their staying power when group efforts fail to produce results."

When a team of individuals share the belief that through their unified efforts, they can overcome challenges and produce intended results, groups *are* more effective. For example, when neighbors share the belief that they can unite to overcome crime, there is significantly less violence.[5] In business, when team members hold positive beliefs about the team's capabilities, creativity and productivity increase.[6]

There are three core attributes necessary to develop collective efficacy:[7]

1. Each person needs to have confidence about their ability and disposition to successfully contribute to a task or accomplish an activity as part of a team (individual efficacy in contributing to the group).

2. Each person needs to have skills in working for themselves and working with everyone in a team (individual efficacy in the skills to work in a team).

3. Each person needs to have confidence or a shared belief in the team's collective capabilities to organize and execute the optimal course of action (individual confidence and skills in the potency power of them working in a group).

Collective efficacy can influence a group's behavior in several ways, including these:

- What they choose to focus on
- How much effort they put in
- Their staying power in the face of extended challenges

This is where professional learning communities came in, transforming isolated teaching practices of the 1960s and earlier years into collaborative, growth-oriented environments. PLCs are intended to empower educators to work together and share insights, strategies, and supports to address the specific assets and needs of their students. Importantly, teams of educators working in PLCs should foster a culture of continuous improvement in which teachers learn from each other, reflect on their practices, and make decisions to enhance student learning. PLCs offer a powerful, research-backed approach for building professional expertise and achieving meaningful, sustained impact in schools.

Video 0.2
Doug explores collective efficacy
qrs.ly/mlghoa7

> **Essential Question**
>
> HOW CAN WE REFINE WHAT PROFESSIONAL LEARNING COMMUNITIES ARE AND HOW THEY IMPACT ADULT AND STUDENT LEARNING?

TWO TRUTHS AND A LIE

Two of these statements are true; one is false. Can you spot the lie?

1. Professional learning communities have been around for such a long time that there is widespread agreement on what a PLC is.

2. Professional learning communities have the potential to raise student learning and student achievement.

3. Although professional learning communities are widely used in schools, teacher preparation programs rarely teach about them or make use of them.

Professional learning communities have been around a long time. However, an overreliance on passed-down traditions has resulted in a patchwork of practices that often do not result in the intended impact. In fact, one research group who conducted a systematic review of the literature on PLCs called it "a meaningless label" because of the lack of a universally understood definition of what it means to function as a learning community.[8] Consequently, the first statement is the lie.

The second statement, which is true, raises an important point: PLCs have the potential to positively impact student learning—but it is not a given.[9] Teams can be hampered by vagueness in their purpose, their goals, and the processes they use to achieve those goals.

Unfortunately, the third statement is also true. Nearly fifty years after PLCs were first introduced to the field, much of what they are and do still seems to rely more on local customs based on the school's culture (i.e., *this is the way we have always done things*) than on actual research, which is what should actually shape a school's professional culture. Further, it is uncommon for teacher preparation programs to discuss collaboration or host PLCs of preservice teachers.[10]

With all of this in mind, it is important to recognize that there is a growing body of evidence about effective structures and protocols that increase the impact PLCs have on students. Returning to the teacher isolation days of the 1950s and 1960s is not desirable, nor is attending useless meetings. Instead, we need to identify and implement what is known about effective PLCs to ensure that they have the intended impact.

WHAT DEFINES AN EFFECTIVE PROFESSIONAL LEARNING COMMUNITY?

In an effective PLC, educators work together to analyze data, examine student work, and share effective teaching strategies, which creates a culture of continuous improvement within the school. The structure promotes open communication, fosters trust among colleagues, and encourages collective problem-solving, allowing teachers to grow professionally in a supportive and reflective environment. We love the following definition, which beautifully sums up the work of high-functioning, high-impact professional learning communities: "knowledge sharing, knowledge creation, the development of new practices and the joint trial and refinement of these practices."[11] Thus PLCs have two complementary purposes:

- Enhancing educators' skills and effectiveness
- Improving student learning outcomes

At the heart of every PLC is a focus on student learning. Team members work together to identify and address the specific needs of their students. PLCs often follow a cycle of inquiry, where teachers set learning goals, collect and analyze data, and implement targeted strategies based on their findings. Importantly, the adults also learn as part of this iterative process; educators continually assess and adjust their approaches based on the evidence gathered. Beyond improving student learning, PLCs aim to create a shared vision and set of values within a school, establishing norms for collaboration and accountability that strengthen the school's professional culture. In doing so, the PLC becomes a mechanism for aligning individual teachers' goals with the broader mission of the school, ensuring that everyone is working in unison toward the same high standards for students.

ASK A BOT

To help align the PLC goals to your school's goals, you might seek assistance from generative AI by using the following frame:

> Here are my school's goals for this year: [**INSERT SCHOOL GOALS**]. Do the goals for our PLC align with these school goals and reflect our core values, such as [***INSERT VALUES, SUCH AS HIGH STANDARDS FOR ALL STUDENTS***]? Provide suggestions on how we can ensure alignment and strengthen the connection between our PLC goals and the broader school vision.

For teachers, the benefits of participating in a PLC are numerous and impactful. PLCs provide a space for educators to collaborate and learn from one another, breaking down the traditional isolation that often comes with teaching. By engaging in meaningful discussions and examining real classroom data, teachers develop a deeper understanding of effective instructional practices and gain new insights they might not have discovered alone. This collaborative approach also helps reduce isolation, as teachers feel supported by their peers and motivated by shared successes. Additionally, PLCs allow teachers to grow professionally by engaging in reflective practices that improve both their skills and their confidence. In a well-functioning PLC, teachers are empowered to take ownership of their professional growth and are better equipped to adapt to the challenges of a diverse, dynamic educational landscape, ultimately leading to a more engaged and effective teaching workforce. In fact, one of the major benefits of professional learning communities is that they can foster teacher agency.[12]

This last point is an especially important one. *Teacher agency* refers to the capacity of teachers to make intentional, autonomous decisions about their practice to best support their students' learning. It involves the ability to adapt, innovate, and take ownership of instructional choices, grounded in professional expertise and knowledge of students' needs. When teachers have agency, they feel empowered to contribute to school decisions, continuously improve their practice, and drive positive change in their classrooms and beyond.

Investigation cycles are essential because they serve as the drivers of professional learning communities. They provide a structured, continuous process for examining and improving teaching practices to enhance student learning. Through these cycles of inquiry, teachers collaboratively set focused goals, collect and analyze data, implement instructional strategies, and reflect on the outcomes. This iterative process allows educators to make data-driven decisions and adapt their approaches based on what is working or what needs adjustment.

Video 0.3
Nancy explores the impact of PLC+ on teacher agency
qrs.ly/I5ghoab

By engaging in regular investigation cycles, PLCs create a culture of continuous improvement where learning is constantly evolving based on evidence rather than assumptions. This approach not only builds collective expertise within the PLC but also fosters a deep sense of accountability and shared commitment to achieving the best possible outcomes for students.

NOTES

QUICK START

	I can start this tomorrow	I can begin this month	I need to discuss this with others	Resources needed
Ask others about the history of professional learning communities in your school or district.				
Reflect on any previous experiences you have had in professional learning communities. When were they effective and when were they not useful?				
Identify the ways that data and evidence of student learning are used in professional learning communities.				
Make a list of the "passed-down traditions" in your PLC and evaluate whether they align with the purpose and goals of a professional learning community.				

(Continued)

(Continued)

	I can start this tomorrow	I can begin this month	I need to discuss this with others	Resources needed
As a team, read the section "What Defines an Effective Professional Learning Community?" and collaborate to establish a shared understanding of what a PLC should and should not be.				
Review the core attributes necessary to develop collective efficacy. Identify specific ways you can contribute to fostering it with your team. For example, you might modify your language to emphasize team success (e.g., "We can solve this together") or encourage collaborative problem-solving when challenges arise.				
Take time to reflect on the collective success of your PLC team. Collectively acknowledge wins, such as implementing an instructional practice or using data to inform practice.				
Discuss examples of successful collaboration and analyze what made those moments effective.				

online resources | Available for download at **https://companion.corwin.com/courses/PLC**

WHAT GETS IN THE WAY OF PROFESSIONAL LEARNING COMMUNITIES?

Conventional practices regarding professional learning communities often stray far from what they were intentioned to do:

- Knowledge sharing
- Knowledge creation
- Development of new practices
- Joint trial and refinement of these practices

Instead, PLCs often operate as isolated teams, rarely (if ever) interacting or learning from other teams in their school. Even more rare are teams that operate among schools. Unfortunately, this silo approach prevents the formation of productive networks, which effective professional learning communities can actually foster. Before we continue, let's briefly examine some of the barriers that can prevent PLCs from working together as high-performing teams.

A LACK OF UNDERSTANDING ABOUT WHAT PROFESSIONAL LEARNING COMMUNITIES ARE

In short, the professional learning community is the school: teams of teachers and leaders working synergistically. Teams operate within the school and contribute to the collective knowledge and practices of the entire community. Yet far too often the team acts as an isolated unit of analysis, not as a cohesive unit across the school. And, unfortunately, when teams are isolated from one another, innovation is thwarted, and the system is structured to maintain silos of excellence.

When teachers work together, they can reduce or eliminate the within-school differences in students' learning. An international study of science performance in sixty-eight countries reported that the variance (the spread between the highest- and lowest-achieving students) is far larger within a school than between schools. Of all the countries studied, the variance in US schools was among the highest, accounting for 80 percent of the differences (the international average was 69 percent).[13] Imagine the impact that this has on students' learning, especially those unlucky enough to be assigned teachers who have no peer support and who are trying their best to implement effective practices. This variation is simply not fair, and it results in differential impacts on student learning.

Marc Tucker, former president of the National Center on Education and the Economy, attributed this wide variation within schools partially to how schools are structured, with little opportunity for teachers to spend time in each other's classrooms working together in teams to solve problems, and with limited chances for new teachers to learn from experts in their own schools.[14] Without regularly scheduled events such as learning walks, without investigation cycles focused on joint trial and refinement of practices, and without school networks to share findings across the school community, change is left to chance.

A LACK OF CLARITY AND SHARED PURPOSE

When team members aren't aligned on goals or lack a clear vision for what they want to accomplish, their efforts often become fragmented. Without a common understanding of the purpose, each member may interpret the work differently, leading to varied priorities and a diluted focus. This lack of alignment can make it challenging to achieve a collective impact on student progress, as members pull in different directions or struggle to prioritize effectively. Schools that mandate a particular focus for the professional learning community, but fail to build a strong rationale for that focus, risk leaving teams in the unenviable position of going through the motions without true intention. Even worse, when the focus is vague and repetitive (e.g., "Our focus this year is on raising test scores in reading and math"), a hodgepodge of strategies is likely to emerge. And don't even get us started about the utter waste of waiting until the fall of the following school year to determine whether your actions resulted in a positive impact.

A LACK OF SUFFICIENT COLLABORATION TIME AND STRUCTURE

Teachers are already stretched thin with daily responsibilities, and without dedicated time for collaborative planning, analyzing data, and discussing instructional strategies, time use can devolve into a series of hurried check-ins rather than productive, reflective meetings. Additionally, without clear agendas or norms for collaboration, meetings may lack focus, leading to frustration among members who feel their time is not used effectively. A high-performing team requires dedicated time with purposeful structures in place to keep the work meaningful and aligned to shared goals.

CONFUSION ABOUT COOPERATION AND COLLABORATION

Shirley Hord's research highlights a critical distinction between teams that work cooperatively and those that work collaboratively. She uses this metaphor: "Dating is a cooperative venture, while marriage is a collaborative one."[15] Cooperative teams can be less successful than collaborative teams because their members may divide tasks and work independently, each responsible for a specific piece of the whole. Although they might come together periodically to share progress, cooperative teams often lack a deep, collective commitment to shared goals about student learning (versus simply getting some required tasks done). Members may focus on their individual successes and struggles, which are eventually combined, but their work remains largely isolated.

In contrast, truly collaborative teams engage in ongoing, interdependent work toward a common challenge. They build shared knowledge, examine data together, and engage in reflective dialogue, continuously adjusting their strategies based on insights from the group. Collaborative teams are committed to shared accountability for results, which means every member is invested not only in their own success but also in the success of the entire group. This level of collaboration fosters a stronger, more unified approach to improving student outcomes, as each member's expertise and insights contribute to collective progress.

NOTES

QUICK START

	I can start this tomorrow	I can begin this month	I need to discuss this with others	Resources needed
Talk with colleagues to learn their perspectives about what gets in the way of a productive professional learning community. Does their feedback align with barriers discussed in this section?				
Identify the existing schedule for PLC team meetings. Name the current focus of your PLC team.				
Identify ways to optimize the use of collaboration time, such as using clear agendas and establishing norms for meetings.				
Reflect on your team's interactions with other teams in your school. Are there any opportunities to collaborate with other teams? Brainstorm ways to engage in cross-team sharing sessions.				
Review your current PLC goals and discuss how they directly align with student success. Are your goals clear enough to drive collective action? Consider revising them if necessary to focus on tangible student outcomes.				

online resources — Available for download at **https://companion.corwin.com/courses/PLC**

WHAT SETS PLC+ APART? INVESTIGATION CYCLES

Investigation cycles, which are a systematic process for collecting, analyzing, and sharing evidence to help organizations improve, drive the PLC+ school. You may have noticed that we used the plural—investigation *cycles*—because effective professional learning communities are nimble and responsive. The common challenge your team chooses to pursue will influence how long a cycle should occur, but we recommend cycles of six to twelve weeks so that teams can learn, innovate, and replicate success quickly.[16] As we have suggested, waiting an entire school year to view state test scores to see whether the professional learning community is having an impact is simply too long. We don't have time for that. We teach with a sense of urgency, and we should collaborate with a sense of urgency, too.

As we have noted earlier, there are five iterative questions that propel each investigation cycle:[17]

1. Where are we going?
2. Where are we now?
3. How do we move learning forward?
4. What did we learn today?
5. Who benefited and who did not?

These questions—and the modules that explore them in this book—are nonlinear in the sense that they *do not* need to be completed in a lockstep fashion, with the first week devoted to the first question, the second week devoted to the second question, and so on. In practice, elements of one or more of these questions emerge as teams move through the cycles. Each question encourages educators to focus on purposeful collaboration, adult-informed and student-centered learning, and evidence-based improvement strategies. These questions serve as a structured approach for teams to assess, reflect on, and refine their instructional practices in a way that directly supports student achievement. By using these questions thoughtfully, the entire professional learning community can stay aligned with their goals and ensure that their actions are data informed and responsive to students' needs. Let's briefly examine each question in more detail.

WHERE ARE WE GOING?

This question invites educators to focus on teacher clarity and establish clear learning intentions and success criteria for students. It emphasizes the importance of having a shared understanding of the intended learning outcomes for students, ensuring that everyone is moving toward a common target. By defining where students should go, the PLC creates a foundation for setting high expectations and aligning teaching strategies. This step also involves identifying key standards, skills, and knowledge that students are expected to develop, which allows educators to plan their lessons and assessments around a unified vision. Further, it prompts teams to calibrate their expectations, such that the activities, assignments, and assessments contain an appropriate level of academic rigor.

WHERE ARE WE NOW?

This question reminds PLCs to assess and reflect on the current state of student learning by analyzing data and student work. As a team, educators determine the students' starting points, strengths, and learning goals so that they can best make use of the learners' strengths and teach in the spaces between what students already know and what they need to know. Through data analysis, educators gain insight into individual and collective progress, allowing them to design future instruction and assessment to meet students' specific needs. Reflecting on current performance also helps teachers recognize any barriers to learning that may hinder students' progress, such as skill gaps or misconceptions, making this a crucial step in shaping effective interventions.

HOW DO WE MOVE LEARNING FORWARD?

Based on data from the previous question, educators select instructional strategies and interventions to bridge the gap between students' current abilities and the desired outcomes. This question encourages teams to explore, select, and implement evidence-based practices that have been shown to accelerate learning. It also provides a unique focus, especially compared to conventional models that overemphasize talk about curriculum and assessment, leaving any discussion of instruction conspicuously absent. By focusing on actionable steps, members collaboratively identify instructional approaches that will provide enrichment, targeted support, and scaffolding. This phase includes implementing learning walks to share best practices and adjusting instructional plans based on ongoing formative assessments to ensure all students continue progressing.

WHAT DID WE LEARN TODAY?

This question encourages teams to reflect on the effectiveness of their actions and to adjust practices as needed. It allows teachers to reflect on their learning from peers during team meetings and from students as they collect and analyze evidence. Reflection is crucial for educators to examine the immediate impact of their instruction on student learning. By discussing what went well and where improvements are needed, teachers can make data-informed decisions to refine their teaching. Continuous reflection strengthens the professional analysis skills of experienced and novice educators and is another unique element of the PLC+ model.[18] Reflection enables teams to be more adaptable and responsive, ensuring that instructional practices are not static but evolve based on students' progress and feedback from the learning environment.

WHO BENEFITED AND WHO DID NOT?

This final question focuses attention on the differential attainment of students within the learning process. Keep in mind the evidence we mentioned earlier: Variance *within* a school is often greater than the variance *between* schools.[19] This question encourages teachers to examine the distribution of learning outcomes and to consider whether all students, particularly those from marginalized or underperforming groups, are advancing. By identifying which students may have been left behind, teams can identify barriers that hindered progress and prioritize interventions that support equitable learning opportunities. This focus helps educators to ensure that all students benefit from high-quality instruction and fosters both individual and collective efficacy for all members of the professional learning community.

Video 0.4
Doug highlights the investigation cycle
qrs.ly/fkghoaf

NOTES

QUICK START

	I can start this tomorrow	I can begin this month	I need to discuss this with others	Resources needed
List the questions you currently use to drive your PLC investigation cycles and compare them to the five guiding questions used in PLC+.				
Consider how conversations about instruction are incorporated into your current PLC processes. Do teams discussed evidence-based practices?				
Ask your administrator about variance in test scores within your school. You may consider the variance within your grade level or school with others in the state or country.				
Consider dedicating PLC time to collectively writing or analyzing intended learning outcomes for students.				

	I can start this tomorrow	I can begin this month	I need to discuss this with others	Resources needed
Discuss any identified barriers to student progress, such as gaps in foundational skills or lack of engagement, and brainstorm strategies for addressing them.				
Analyze recent assessments and student work to determine current student performance. Identify trends, strengths, and areas needing improvement across the group.				
Reflect on the common instructional strategies your team has developed to support student learning. What shared research-based instructional moves are consistently used across PLC member classrooms? How do individual teaching styles shape the implementation of these strategies while still maintaining their research-based integrity?				

online resources Available for download at **https://companion.corwin.com/courses/PLC**

WHAT SETS PLC+ APART? FOUR CROSSCUTTING VALUES

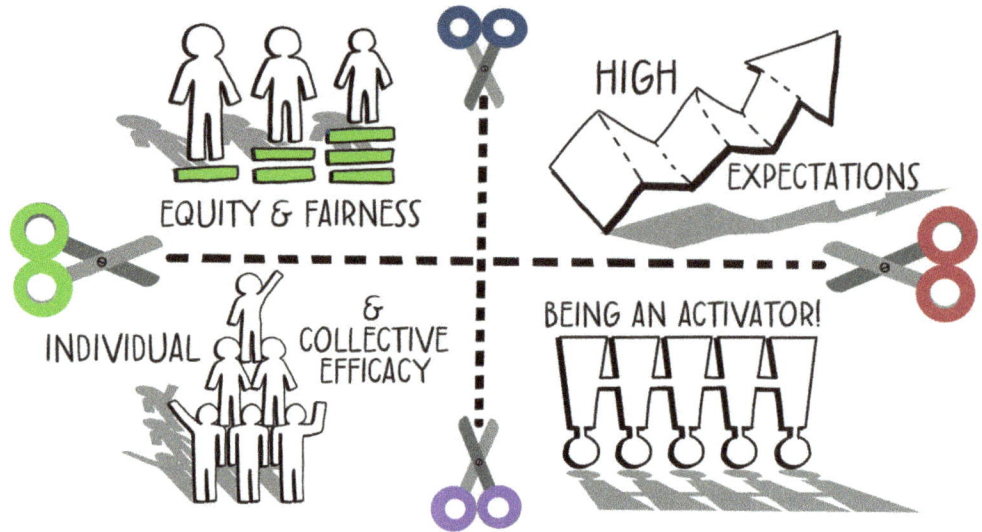

Crosscutting values are essential throughout the investigation cycle because they provide a consistent foundation that guides every stage of collaborative inquiry and decision-making. These values—equity and fairness, individual and collective efficacy, high expectations, and activation—shape how PLC+ teams approach their work, ensuring that their efforts remain purposeful, inclusive, and focused on impactful outcomes for all students. By embedding these values into each step of the cycle, from analyzing data to implementing strategies, teams are more likely to create a unified culture that supports sustained improvement. These guiding principles not only influence what actions are taken but also inform the mindset and commitment each member brings to the table, fostering a supportive, results-driven environment where every student has the opportunity to succeed. Let's examine each crosscutting value in more detail.

EQUITY AND FAIRNESS

The value of equity and fairness is foundational in the PLC+ model, emphasizing the need for fair and just opportunities for every student. This value calls for teams to continuously examine and address disparities in educational access and outcomes. *Equity* is about acknowledging and removing systemic barriers, adapting teaching methods, and ensuring that every student—regardless of background or current level of performance—has the support they need to succeed. *Fairness* requires impartial and just treatment without favoritism. In other words, we have unconditional positive regard for all our students. Fairness does not mean giving everyone the same thing, but rather making decisions about what individual students need. By embedding equity and Liberatory Design into their practices, PLC+ teams are better equipped to make fair decisions and engage in decision-driven data collection that prioritize all students' growth and learning needs.

HIGH EXPECTATIONS

High expectations are essential in establishing a culture of rigorous academic standards and mutual accountability. In the PLC+ model, high expectations extend to both teachers and students, with educators setting ambitious goals for student learning and maintaining confidence in students' ability to reach them. This value also drives team members to push one another toward growth, encouraging reflection and strengthening instructional practices. By holding high expectations, PLC+ teams create an environment where each student is challenged to excel and where teachers are committed to continually raising the bar. Importantly, high expectations paired with high support create an equitable learning environment and serve as the recipe for motivating young people.[20]

INDIVIDUAL AND COLLECTIVE EFFICACY

This third crosscutting value refers to the shared belief, supported by evidence of impact, that together teachers have the skills to positively influence student outcomes.[21] When educators have a strong sense of collective efficacy, they feel empowered to overcome obstacles and work toward meaningful change. This value encourages teachers to support one another in both challenges and successes, fostering a strong, unified approach to teaching. Collective efficacy strengthens the team's resilience, as teachers understand that their combined efforts have the potential to significantly impact students, bolstering their motivation and commitment to achieving shared goals.

ACTIVATORS

This last crosscutting value focuses on taking proactive steps to influence and drive collaborative practices among adults that improve student outcomes. Activators within a PLC+ setting actively seek out and implement strategies that help the team arrive at agreements, propose approaches, monitor progress, and adjust methods based on data and student needs. Each member of the team is an activator of each other's thinking, regardless of experience or expertise. By acting as activators, members support one another not only in making evidence-based instructional decisions but also in spreading innovation across the professional learning community.

Video 0.5
Nancy highlights the crosscutting values
qrs.ly/cfghoah

QUICK START

	I can start this tomorrow	I can begin this month	I need to discuss this with others	Resources needed
Consider the ways in which your PLC delivers on the promise of equity.				
Discuss how high expectations are conveyed in the classroom.				
Describe the efficacy of team members and the collective.				
Explore the role of the activator and how team meetings are facilitated and monitored.				
Examine student data for disparities based on race, socioeconomic status, gender, disability, and other factors.				
Collaborate with a colleague with the intention of examining lessons for cultural responsiveness.				
Acknowledge and celebrate the progress made toward high expectations, both for students and for team members.				
Create a shared definition for what equity means at your site or in your PLC.				
Reflect on your role as an activator within your PLC. Think about the tools in your toolkit that you use to support collaboration and innovation. For example, consider what strategies you use to help your team arrive at agreements, even when perspectives differ. How do you encourage the team to explore and embrace new approaches? What approaches do you use to respectfully question long-standing practices or assumptions?				

online resources Available for download at **https://companion.corwin.com/courses/PLC**

WHAT SETS PLC+ APART? A LIBERATORY DESIGN APPROACH

Liberatory Design is both a process and a practice to address persistent inequities in complex systems in order to foster transformative change.[22] By merging the principles of human-centered design thinking with the principles of equity, this approach seeks to elevate empathy, creativity, and iterative experimentation to shift persistent patterns of inequitable outcomes and experiences. Its practice is grounded in a set of key mindsets intended to achieve the following:

- Support practitioners to explicitly and intentionally attend to trust and relationship building
- Attend to and shift power dynamics
- Recognize the ways that systemic oppression is operating in complex ways to produce inequitable outcomes

In centering liberation, PLC+ encourages educators not only to imagine new solutions but also to identify barriers that impede equitable access, participation, and outcomes—and then design approaches to overcome those barriers. The critical stances and process guidance offered by the Liberatory Design approach support PLC+ participants to (1) learn through doing, (2) partner with each other as well as with students and other community members, and (3) ultimately create the conditions necessary for collective liberation and create sustainable improvements.

There are three major components that comprise the Liberatory Design approach:

1. *Liberatory Design mindsets* offer stances and values that individuals and groups can invoke individually and collectively in their design, leadership, and collaboration to work toward liberatory outcomes.

2. *Liberatory Design modes*, depicted in the flower graphic on the next page, offer a variety of ways to guide and structure your group's design process.

It's important to note that even though the petals of the flower suggest a cycle, Liberatory Design is nonlinear and iterative. Your team can use these modes as needed in the context of your investigation cycle.

3. The *National Equity Project's (2024) Leading for Equity Framework*[23], which guides Liberatory Design, equips educational leaders to address complex, systemic inequities and take purposeful action to foster youth and community thriving.

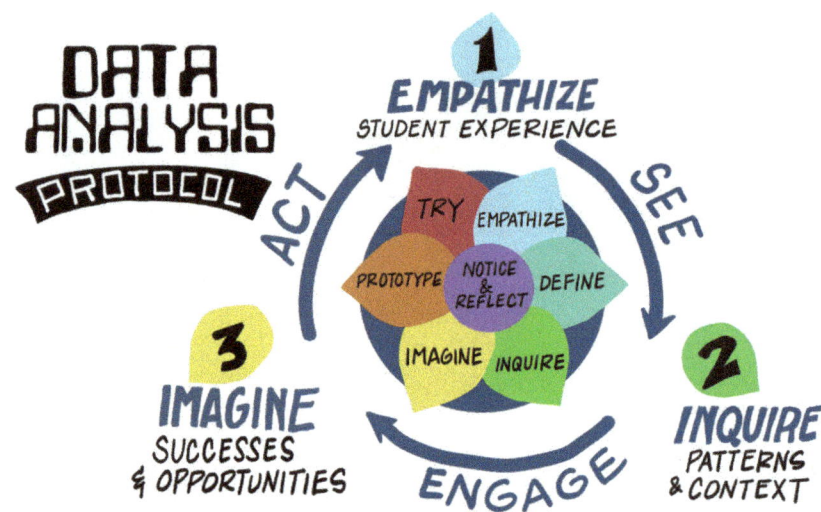

Adapted from "Liberatory Design for Equity" by the National Equity Project. Derived from Anaissie, T., Cary, V., Clifford, D., Malarkey, T. & Wise, S. (2021). *Liberatory Design*. www.liberatorydesign.com.

At the heart of Liberatory Design are the modes of Notice and Reflect, which appear at the center of the flower. These modes provide an anchor for teams to recenter themselves throughout their work and to build greater self-awareness along with a capacity to shift how they're working.

Specifically, *Notice* helps PLC+ team members practice self-awareness and situational awareness:

- **Self-awareness**: Who are we as team (e.g., identities, experiences, history)? How are we doing (e.g., emotions, relationships)? What intentions do we want to bring to this next part of our work together? How might we need to shift how we're working together?

- **Situational awareness**: What is our context now? What has shifted? What feels important to anticipate?

Reflect helps PLC+ team members pause and adjust:

- **Pause**: Teams pause to reflect on our actions and equity impact, as well as our emotions and relationships.

- **Adjust**: Teams adjust our direction, our strategy, and/or how we're working together.

As shown in the figure, a key element of Liberatory Design is its emphasis on *empathize* and *define* practices. These practices prioritize relationship building and inquiry approaches designed to result in a deep understanding of the lived experiences of the people most affected by inequities—as well as the people who unwittingly contribute to the conditions and practices holding those inequities in place. Unlike traditional design thinking, which often centers on end users or clients, Liberatory Design emphasizes authentic engagement with communities. This approach requires teams to do the following:

- Actively listen
- Validate personal and collective experiences
- Ensure that the perspectives of those most impacted guide the process

Because this empathetic grounding allows for a more comprehensive and accurate identification of challenges, it helps your team develop solutions that genuinely address root causes rather than symptoms.

Another significant aspect of Liberatory Design is its iterative process, which combines creative ideation with critical reflection to ensure that your team's progress is in continuous alignment with equity goals. This reflection prompts your team to examine assumptions, question dominant narratives, and refine solutions based on learning with and from the impacted communities. The iterative nature of this model allows teams to remain adaptable, learning together and correcting course as needed. Adaptability is crucial for advancing student and adult learning because it encourages students and teachers to treat challenges as learning opportunities, and it encourages teams to refine their strategies to better serve the communities they aim to support.

In a PLC+ community, there may be imbalances of power between new and veteran teachers, BIPOC teachers and white teachers, and department leads and those without formal leadership positions. These imbalances impact who feels agency to speak up, who is listened to, which ideas get considered, and which ideas are disregarded. Liberatory Design's emphasis on cocreation and shared leadership further advances the PLC+ community efforts by encouraging groups to prioritize time and intention to create an inclusive environment where power imbalances and challenging dynamics are named and tended; this helps ensure that many voices have the opportunity to actively shape decision-making.

By decentralizing power in order to value contributions from all, the Liberatory Design approach promotes shared leadership and amplifies the voices of those who might otherwise be sidelined in traditional design processes. As a result, the outcomes are more representative, more innovative, and more effective as they draw from a broader range of insights and experiences, especially those of the people who are most impacted by the challenges being addressed. This collaborative framework ultimately empowers teams to address complex challenges in ways that are both empathetic and impactful.

Consider this example of a high school PLC using the Liberatory Design framework to guide their conversations after they observe unequal patterns of participation during group projects in social studies classes. The team uses the Liberatory Design framework to take the following steps:

1. **Empathize Mode**: The PLC conducts empathy interviews with students, especially students who are most impacted by the challenges the PLC intends to address, asking them to share their experiences with group projects. They discover that some students feel their ideas are dismissed or overshadowed by peers, while others express a lack of confidence in participating due to language barriers or limited prior knowledge.

2. **Define Mode**: The team defines the problem as "unequal participation in group projects, caused by inequitable group dynamics and insufficient scaffolding."

3. **Ideation and Implementation:** The team decides to take action, discussing equitable participation goals with students and restructuring group tasks to include individual accountability.

Video 0.6
Overview of Liberatory Design
qrs.ly/coghoaj

ASK A BOT

Sometimes, despite our best intentions, we may overlook our own areas of unawareness. This can lead us to observe situations and unintentionally phrase things in ways that aren't constructive or that may cause harm. To approach challenges with greater empathy and understanding, consider using AI to help reform your group's observation. AI can help your team express issues in a way that avoids stereotypes and seeks deeper understanding. To begin, try using this prompt:

> We are observing [**INSERT ISSUE HERE, E.G., *PARTICULAR GROUPS OF STUDENTS ARE NOT APPLYING THEMSELVES OR ENGAGED IN LEARNING***]. Can you help us rephrase this issue in a more empathetic and solution-focused way? Additionally, suggest strategies or questions we can use to better understand the underlying causes from the students' perspectives.

NOTES

QUICK START

	I can start this tomorrow	I can begin this month	I need to discuss this with others	Resources needed
How do the PLC teams at your school see, engage, and act? Identify processes that are used to accomplish each of these.				
Consider the impact of systems thinking, through a Liberatory Design lens, on your colleagues and your students.				
Create opportunities for all voices to provide feedback during key decision-making moments. Use anonymous surveys, independent writing before sharing, or rotating leadership roles to encourage participation from all voices.				
Create a space for both individual and group reflection on how inclusivity and shared leadership are being practiced.				

(Continued)

(Continued)

	I can start this tomorrow	I can begin this month	I need to discuss this with others	Resources needed
Pay attention to the power dynamics that play out in your team meeting. Ask yourself questions like these: What patterns do I see with regard to who speaks and who doesn't? How do our meeting structures, locations, and processes support shared power or reinforce imbalances of power? Are all perspectives valued? Are we living up to our commitment for shared decision-making?				
During family conferences or other family engagement opportunities, ask family members these questions: What are your values? How do these values connect to the goals you have for your child this year? What is the most important thing you hope they achieve during this phase of their schooling? What is happening at school that is supporting accomplishing this? What is happening at school that is blocking this?				
Commit to listening to diverse voices—including students and families—when making key decisions about teaching, learning, and equity initiatives. Incorporate structures and processes that cultivate conditions for those from nondominant cultures to authentically participate and collaborate on key decisions.				
Work collaboratively to identify and list the groups whose perspectives should be included to ensure equitable and informed decision-making.				

online resources Available for download at **https://companion.corwin.com/courses/PLC**

WHAT SETS PLC+ APART? THE COMMON CHALLENGE

Shared goals drive the actions any team takes, whether it is competitive (e.g., winning the soccer match) or collaborative (e.g., gaining market share in the third quarter). In education, the shared goal, broadly, is to improve and accelerate student learning. But without fully understanding existing barriers and strengths, it is nearly impossible for teams to determine what actions will remove those barriers and leverage those strengths. Liberatory Design offers process guidance to help teams identify common challenges and envision new, liberatory realities to work toward.

Specifically, the Liberatory Design mode labeled *define* helps teams develop a point of view about the needs of the community and the common challenges that must be addressed to meet those needs. PLC+ teams identify a common challenge by creating a statement about the community's current status, which serves to clarify exactly what problem the team will address. These statements are often the product of the first two questions in the investigation cycle: *Where are we going?* and *Where are we now?* Here are some examples of effective common challenges:

- Multilingual learners at our school tend to excel on the speaking and listening portions of the state's language assessment, but they often struggle with the reading and writing portions.

- Students' skills and habits in terms of study skills can be expanded.

- We want to strengthen our innovative technology usage in our teaching.

Notice all these common challenges are phrased as statements rather than as questions, and they are voiced in a way that identifies the present level of performance. Further, they are easy to remember, which improves clarity and commitment to the common challenge. Also note that these challenges aren't SMART goals, which often require several meetings to agree on and are frequently *given to* teachers rather than *developed by* teachers. SMART goals may also be created to cover an entire year, whereas common challenges focus on the current issue the team is facing.

When teams define a common challenge, they help ensure that discussions remain focused on student-centered outcomes rather than veering into general teaching practices or administrative tasks. This focus is essential because the primary goal of PLC+ is to improve student learning by analyzing and responding to data on student performance. When educators center their

Video 0.7
Nancy highlights the common challenge
qrs.ly/ctghoan

conversations around how well students are achieving specific goals, they can more effectively identify what instructional strategies are working and where adjustments are needed. Most important, this approach allows PLC+ teams to gauge their impact as they gather the evidence needed for the formation of each common challenge.

NOTES

QUICK START

	I can start this tomorrow	I can begin this month	I need to discuss this with others	Resources needed
Identify a common challenge that may serve to unite your team.				
Consider the difference between framing this as a SMART goal versus a common challenge.				
Practice rephrasing challenges as statements and not questions. Use concise, focused statements that clearly outline the current status of student performance.				
Review the shared common challenge your PLC has developed. Reflect on the clarity of the common challenge and whether or not the challenge provides a focused direction for your team's collaborative efforts.				
Bring relevant data to your next PLC meeting. Collaboratively analyze the data and identify the progress made toward meeting the common challenge.				
Reflect on how a student's entire school experience impacts academic outcomes. What are the factors that contribute to students' social and emotional well-being?				

Available for download at **https://companion.corwin.com/courses/PLC**

EMPATHY MAPPING

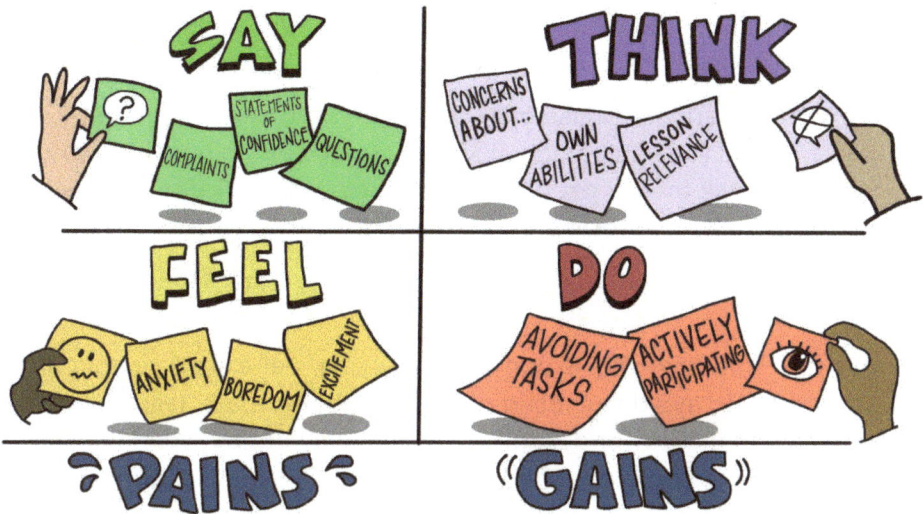

The call for teachers to *empathize*, which is also one of the modes of Liberatory Design, asks educators to understand the experiences, emotions, and motivations of those who are most impacted by the challenges that educators are hoping to address. Engaging in empathy work allows educators to gain a rich understanding of the students and communities they serve. When done with intention and from a place of love, respect, and curiosity, empathy work can support educators, students, and other stakeholders to develop deeper levels of relational trust. While there are many different ways to empathize, we will highlight empathy mapping as an effective approach to help the school community gain a deeper understanding of their students' perspectives, emotions, and needs, which makes it especially valuable for professional learning communities who are working to improve instructional practices.

An empathy map is a tool developed at the Stanford d.school that visually represents what students say, think, feel, and do, allowing educators to step outside of their own assumptions and view learning challenges through the students' eyes. Empathy maps can highlight areas where students might be experiencing obstacles or frustrations, and they can uncover potential motivations and aspirations that can guide more student-centered instruction.

Using empathy maps in a PLC+ allows teachers to create a collective picture of their students' experiences, which is invaluable when interpreting data and planning interventions. Rather than only focusing on numbers and scores, an empathy map brings in qualitative insights that provide deeper context to quantitative data. These insights enable the team to identify and discuss strategies that respond to students' emotional and motivational needs, not just their academic ones.

To create an empathy map, team members first gather information from students, including informal interviews, about a particular topic that the professional learning community is interested in improving. Here are some examples of topic ideas:

- Ask students about a time when they felt success or when something was challenging. Ask them how they felt, what they did, and what they wished would have happened.
- Ask students about a sense of belonging in school. Ask them what it means to feel like you belong at school, and what the best and worst parts of that are. Ask them what suggestions they would offer to new teachers to help all students feel like they belong.
- Ask students what advice they would give to younger students.

Note that when empathy work is done poorly, it can feel extractive, tokenizing, and transactional. To avoid stumbling onto this negative path, teams should remain attentive to the power dynamics that can play out between teachers and students, which can be amplified when differences in race, gender, class, or sexual orientation are present. In particular, it is important for teams to take time to set intentions about how the educators doing the empathy mapping hope to be experienced by students and to generate ideas about actions that will support these intentions. When done well, empathy mapping and other empathy work will strengthen relationships and deepen understanding.

During the process of empathy mapping, the professional learning community gathers to share what students say, think, feel, and do in relation to the topic. They create a blank, four-quadrant map using the headings shown in the previous illustration and then they fill in the quadrants based on the students' responses to the empathy-based questions. For instance, in the quadrant with the heading "Say," teachers would share what students verbally express, such as complaints, questions, or statements of confidence. In the quadrants marked "Think" and "Feel," teachers explore what students might be thinking but not saying—perhaps concerns about their own abilities or the relevance of the lesson—as well as emotions such as anxiety, boredom, or excitement are documented. Then, in the section marked "Do," the team would document visible behaviors, like avoiding tasks or actively participating. The "Pains" and "Gains" categories on the map invite participants to note voiced or unvoiced concerns and hopes.

It is also a best practice for educators to circle back to the students who participated to share what the team learned from them. This inclusive approach invites students to also make sense of the data gathered, and it helps the team to check that their synthesis of students' perspectives feels accurate and in alignment with what the students hoped the teachers would take away. This is what it means to design *with*, rather than *for*, students.

Empathy mapping is a powerful step toward creating a more responsive, supportive learning environment. By actively considering students' thoughts, emotions, and motivations, teachers can make informed decisions about a common challenge that resonates more deeply. This tool also fosters shared understanding and collaboration within teams and the entire professional learning community, as educators combine their insights to create a fuller picture of their students. In this way, empathy mapping encourages a shift from focusing solely on academic outcomes to seeing and addressing the broader context of student experiences, helping PLC+ teams build instructional practices that are both data informed and deeply empathetic. Through this process, PLC+ teams develop a well-rounded view of student experiences that might not be immediately apparent from data alone.

Video 0.8
Nancy discusses empathy interviews
qrs.ly/oqghoao

NOTES

COMMON CHALLENGE PROTOCOL

The common challenge protocol provides teams with a process to identify their why, or the reason that they spend time together. The common challenge helps teams find purpose in their work together, which is especially important for teams that have members teaching different age groups or content areas.

Purpose: To collaboratively understand and frame a common challenge based on community-defined needs, values, and a comprehensive view of student experiences.

Suggested Time: 45 minutes

STEP 1: Define the Common Challenge (20 minutes)

1. **Share and Reflect on Data (5 minutes)**
   - **Data Presentation:** Present both quantitative data (e.g., assessment results) and qualitative data (e.g., student feedback, observations).
   - **Contextual Inquiry:** Discuss the factors contributing to current outcomes, focusing on student engagement, inclusion, and system-wide patterns that impact learning.

2. **Collaborative Sense Making (10 minutes)**
   - **Identify Needs and Patterns:**
     - Use storytelling and perspective sharing to identify patterns in data and uncover root causes.
     - **Guiding Question:** "What core needs or challenges do students express, and how might these reflect broader patterns in our system?"
   - **Expand the Problem Definition:**
     - Discuss how the challenge might impact different student groups, and frame it to capture diverse needs.
   - **Guiding Questions:**
     - "How has this challenge been shaped by our current structures?"
     - "Who benefits or is disadvantaged by this system, and what are their experiences?"
   - **Document Reflections:** Summarize insights from the discussion to capture a holistic view of the challenge, prioritizing needs that reflect both shared and unique student experiences.

3. **Formulate the Challenge Statement (5 minutes)**
   - Draft a concise challenge statement that reflects the team's understanding of student needs and includes perspectives on accessibility, engagement, and growth.
   - **Example:** "Students generally are not feeling engaged or inspired by the work they are assigned, and they want more opportunities to interact with peers in their learning."

STEP 2: Inquiry Into the Challenge (25 minutes)

1. **Identify Gaps in Understanding (5 minutes)**
   - **Map Out Uncertainties:** Each team member reflects on aspects of the challenge they feel uncertain about or wish to explore further.

- **Guiding Questions:**
  - "What do we still need to understand about the student experience regarding this challenge?"
  - "Are there any assumptions about student needs we should examine?"

2. **Inquiry Planning (10 minutes)**
   - **Explore Safe-to-Fail Actions:**
     - Brainstorm small, low-risk activities that could reveal more information (e.g., piloting a survey, conducting empathy interviews).
     - Focus on methods that encourage student input and support team learning.
   - **Design Questions for Investigation:**
     - **Example:** "What barriers do students identify as impacting their engagement in this area?"
     - **Example:** "How do students and families feel this issue affects their school experience?"
   - **Document Inquiry Actions:** Create a list of specific inquiry steps, and assign roles, ensuring each team member's perspective is valued in the discovery process.

3. **Debrief and Reflect (10 minutes)**
   - **Sense-Making Discussion:** As a team, review findings, focusing on insights that reveal more about the underlying dynamics of the common challenge.
   - **Challenge Statement Reevaluation:** After discussing findings, revisit and refine the common challenge statement if needed.
   - **Plus/Delta Feedback on Inquiry:** Gather reflections on what aspects of the inquiry process were helpful and what adjustments could improve future cycles.

Quality Checklist for the Common Challenge

- [ ] Is the common challenge we developed consequential to students, teachers, and/or families? How do we know?
- [ ] Is it stated in observable and measurable terms?
- [ ] Do the members of the team have a shared understanding of the common challenge? Do those most impacted by this challenge agree with how we have defined the challenge?

Video 0.9
A team works through the Common Challenge protocol
qrs.ly/lyghoau

A COMMON CHALLENGE WITH LIBERATORY DESIGN MODES

As we've noted, the Liberatory Design mode labeled *define* helps teams identify the needs of the community and the key challenges they must address in order to meet those needs. This approach is used whenever teams have gathered sufficient data for their investigation to make decisions about where they will focus their efforts for the investigation cycle. This data are usually the product of the first two questions: *Where are we going?* and *Where are we now?*

This common challenge protocol is designed to aid teams in discussion and decision-making. As with all discussions, yours may vary a bit from the suggested protocol, and that's fine. Further, as your team tries on different strategies to address the challenge and learn from their implementation, you may find that you need to fine-tune the original challenge statement later in the cycle. The key is to always keep in mind the overall purpose of the common challenge: Clearly define the problem and work toward consensus.

Liberatory Design offers a mindset that is essential when discussing the quantitative and qualitative data used: "Share, don't sell." We all have perspectives we are especially passionate about, which means we can err by trying to convince others of the value, rather than inviting them into the process of being collaborators.[24] By staying open to others and avoiding becoming too attached to our ideas, we allow room for the refinement and incorporation of new ideas. As organizational productivity expert Edward Deming noted, "Every system is perfectly designed to get the result that it does."[25] If we want to change the trajectory of student learning, we must be open to multiple perspectives.

The common challenge protocol with Liberatory Design modes is intended to provide time and space for teams to do the hard intellectual and social/emotional work of ideation and creation. Far too often, schools take an all-too-common approach of "ready, fire, aim," which undermines school improvement efforts by rushing to action before the team can take time to consider what problem we are really trying to resolve. In contrast, the protocol offers a process that supports teams to thoughtfully define needs and challenges as well as identify areas that may necessitate deeper inquiry in order to surface the learning needed to effectively understand and address the challenges. The outline on the previous page is set up to show how teams might use the protocol to guide a forty-five-minute common challenge meeting.

CASE IN POINT: A SHALLOW WADE INTO DATA WATERS

The eighth-grade PLC team at Pin Oak Junior High sat around a table in the library, stacks of student data sheets and notebooks scattered across the surface. Sarah Clarkson, the eighth-grade science teacher, sighed as she looked over her notes. Then she admitted, "It just feels like we're always talking about the same things. We identify areas where students struggle, but we never seem to get anywhere. We gather data, but I'm not sure we're really using it effectively."

James Washington, the math teacher, nodded in agreement. "I know what you mean. We talk about proficiency scores and gaps, but we're not really digging into why those gaps are there. It's like we're only scratching the surface. And we only seem to hear from a few of us in these meetings. I feel like we need a new approach if we're really going to help our students."

"Exactly," replied Mia Rodriguez, the English teacher. "We keep saying we want to make things better for everyone, but we don't even know what 'better' looks like for some of our students. I've been thinking about how to bring in more of their voices, maybe get a better sense of their needs beyond test scores." She paused, glancing around the room, and then added, "What if we tried to focus on understanding their experiences instead of just their performance?"

Sarah leaned forward, intrigued. "That might be exactly what we need. Maybe instead of just analyzing the numbers, we could try to understand more about what's driving those numbers."

What's Your Advice?

- How can this team move from simply reviewing data to understanding the root causes of student learning struggles?

- What steps could the team take to make their meetings feel more productive and less repetitive?

- How can the team balance the need to address proficiency gaps with a broader approach to understanding student needs?

Video 0.10
An activator reflects on the case in point
qrs.ly/kqghoaz

Introduction 43

CROSSCUTTING VALUES CHECK

What is the current status of the professional learning community in your school? Consider these reflective questions to spark discussion with colleagues.

Equity and Fairness

- What processes do we have in place to understand who is benefiting and who is not benefiting from our instruction? How are these processes working for us?
- How do we learn about our impact on all students, including those with disabilities, multilingual learners, and advanced learners?
- How do we interrogate variance with regard to student performance and outcomes? What do we attribute to students' personal characteristics? Are these justified?

High Expectations

- How strong are our practices in relation to adherence to grade-level content?
- In what ways do we demonstrate high expectations of all students, including those with disabilities, multilingual learners, and advanced learners?
- How do we support and encourage one another as colleagues? How do we encourage risk-taking in service of learning?

Individual and Collective Efficacy

- How do we uphold high expectations for ourselves in terms of belief about our ability to positively impact the learning of all students?
- What supports are regularly utilized by all teachers (novice, experienced, and expert) to ensure continued professional growth?
- How do we make space to share our learnings with the broader school community and engage the work of other PLC teams?

Activators

- How do we ensure that any and all members are encouraged and supported to be activators, not just the person with the most seniority or highest position?
- Does our team include a range of professionals, including special and general educators, so that we can benefit from different perspectives?
- How do we understand the difference between collaborating and cooperating? What indicators do we see of collaborating on our team? What indicators do we see of cooperation on our team?

SELF-ASSESSMENT

Use the following five statements, one per essential question, for rapid assessment. Read the question and corresponding statement, and then discuss your current state with your PLC+ team. Come to a shared agreement about the current capacity and implementation for each statement.

1. Notice: Where Are We Going?

    We define our expectations through learning intentions and success criteria, and these definitions involve learning progressions over time, moving to the point of equity of access and opportunity for learning for all students.

1	2	3	4	5
Not Begun or Not Initiated	Very Limited Evidence of Capacity	Some Evidence of Capacity	Evidence of Capacity and Limited Evidence of Effective Implementation	Evidence of Capacity and Demonstrated Effective Implementation

   Reflect: Who is "in the know" about our expectations? How have our processes made space for students, families, and educators to co-construct and/or understand these expectations? What do we believe about how much these groups should contribute to defining our expectations?

2. Notice: Where Are We Now?

    We collect and analyze evidence to understand our students, identify equity gaps, challenge bias, and define common challenges that unite our efforts and support collective efficacy.

1	2	3	4	5
Not Begun or Not Initiated	Very Limited Evidence of Capacity	Some Evidence of Capacity	Evidence of Capacity and Limited Evidence of Effective Implementation	Evidence of Capacity and Demonstrated Effective Implementation

   Reflect: What evidence do we collect? What does this evidence support us to see? What are the limitations of this evidence in supporting us to see the unique interests, skills, and talents that our students possess and opportunities to build from those assets in our work to support learners?

3. Notice: How Do We Move Learning Forward?

    We match evidence-based instructional approaches to defined learning needs, assess and increase our own abilities to deliver instruction, and use learning walks and microteaching to move learning forward.

(Continued)

(Continued)

1	2	3	4	5
Not Begun or Not Initiated	Very Limited Evidence of Capacity	Some Evidence of Capacity	Evidence of Capacity and Limited Evidence of Effective Implementation	Evidence of Capacity and Demonstrated Effective Implementation

Reflect: How do make decisions about instructional moves? In what ways do we learn from others about effective practices? How do we draw from Black, Indigenous, and other minoritized and marginalized communities to learn culturally responsive and relevant instructional approaches? Do we believe that we can benefit from these perspectives?

4. Notice: What Did We Learn Today?

   We regularly examine our practice, discuss expectations, identify and act on student needs, and seek to describe elements of our practice that yield, or do not yield, a measurable, positive impact.

1	2	3	4	5
Not Begun or Not Initiated	Very Limited Evidence of Capacity	Some Evidence of Capacity	Evidence of Capacity and Limited Evidence of Effective Implementation	Evidence of Capacity and Demonstrated Effective Implementation

Reflect: How do we understand student needs? What processes do we have that support students to articulate their needs and provide feedback about how our curriculum and pedagogy meet their needs? How do students know we've heard them?

5. Notice: Who Benefitted and Who Did Not?

   We intentionally seek to identify patterns that suggest barriers to learning, monitor progress and achievement for all students, and modify instruction using strategies that include tiered systems, new approaches to instruction, and heightening collective efficacy.

1	2	3	4	5
Not Begun or Not Initiated	Very Limited Evidence of Capacity	Some Evidence of Capacity	Evidence of Capacity and Limited Evidence of Effective Implementation	Evidence of Capacity and Demonstrated Effective Implementation

Reflect: Whose voices have been invited to seek patterns? What might we learn from engaging paraprofessionals, after-school staff, students, and families if we invited them to help identify patterns? What fears or reservations might we be holding in inviting these perspectives? What structural barriers need to be addressed in order to engage these groups authentically?

online resources Available for download at **https://companion.corwin.com/courses/PLC**

NOTICE AND REFLECT

 ## ESSENTIAL QUESTION

How can we refine what our professional learning communities are and how they impact adult and student learning?

THINK ABOUT

- Are we satisfied with our current professional learning community scheme?
- Do we learn from each other as a professional learning community, or is wisdom siloed?
- Are our efforts fair and equitable?
- What are our current strengths, and where do we need to grow?

START – STOP – KEEP

Based on what you learned in this module, answer the questions below.

Start: What practice(s) would you like to start doing?

Stop: What practice(s) would you like to stop doing?

Keep: What practice(s) would you like to keep doing?

1 WHERE ARE WE GOING?

There is some joy in wandering. Perhaps we're sauntering through a park, letting the road take us on a journey. Or we're out for a bike ride, mountain climbing, or strolling through a mall and window shopping. In these cases, the experience is the journey, and we get to encounter things that we may have missed if we were hyperfocused on the destination. But at some point, we want to go home, so we have a clear destination. Consequently, our focus hones in on the efficiency of accomplishing the goal of arriving home safely in as little time as possible.

The learning that occurs in our classrooms often has a clear destination articulated in the standards and curriculum. There may also be prescribed steps and time constraints, including the urgency to ensure that students learn all that they can. Yet we can reconnect to the joy of wandering by remembering that Liberatory Design is about both the journey (process) and the destination (outcomes). En route to the learning destination we may encounter barriers, setbacks, delays, or unexpected complications, but even if we have a few paths to choose from, the learning goal remains constant. We don't alter or differentiate these outcomes. Instead, we focus on the learning journey and the supports required to ensure that students reach the goals. Even if setbacks and delays arise, we remain focused on efficiently and effectively designing the learning journey for students to arrive successfully and safely at their destinations. while preserving the joy of discovery along the way.

Essential Question

HOW CAN TEACHER TEAMS IDENTIFY THE LEARNING JOURNEYS OF THEIR STUDENTS?

Video 1.1
An elementary team discusses question 1
qrs.ly/5qghob2

Video 1.2
A secondary team discusses question 1
qrs.ly/6vghob3

TWO TRUTHS AND A LIE

***Two of these statements are true; one is false.
Can you spot the lie?***

1. Teacher teams should decide what they want students to learn.
2. The learning journey for students needs to align with appropriate grade-level expectations.
3. The foundation for PLC+ is teacher clarity.

Professional learning communities existed long before there were standards. For example, prior to 1997, when the California State Board of Education adopted standards for what every student should learn in every grade, teachers or school systems decided what students needed to learn. As a result, there could be widely different experiences between different classrooms in the same school. PLCs could not have meaningful conversations if each educator was teaching different things, so the logical first question was to agree on what students would learn. Today, however, the content standards reflect what our society has agreed students need to know and be able do to. Consequently, the first statement is the lie. Teams should spend their energy focused not on what students should learn but rather on what the next step in the learning journey will be as students reach proficiency on the standards.

The second statement is an important distinction. In the past, education was very developmentally focused. Teachers taught at their students' current proficiency levels. But teaching a sixth grader the third-grade standards based on their current performance will produce a seventh grader who is ready for fourth grade. Instead, teachers design lessons that provide students access to the thinking and expectations of the grade-level standards and ensure that scaffolding and support make the learning comprehensible. Schools that are able to change the trajectory of students' learning—contributing on average more than one year of learning for each year students are in school—consistently focus on teaching students the appropriate, grade-level standards.[26]

The third statement is also true. Teacher clarity is foundational to the work that teacher teams do. In fact, teacher clarity is the *what* while PLC+ is the *how*. Teacher teams work to understand the standards and develop clarity in terms of the organization of learning; the examples, explanations, and practice offered to students; and the ways in which assessment evidence is collected, analyzed, and valued.[27] As part of this process, teams examine learning progressions and define what successful learning will look like each day for an instructional unit. Teacher team discussions focus on achieving clarity by understanding the expectations of the standards, organizing learning, refining examples and explanations, designing meaningful practice opportunities, and determining how to collect and analyze assessment evidence.

THE STORY BEHIND THE QUESTION (WHERE ARE WE GOING?)

As we have noted, older versions of professional learning communities focused on what students would learn, and teacher teams negotiated among themselves about their goals for students. This led to significant differences in the experiences students had and the eventual success that some students demonstrated. Simply said, it wasn't fair for some students to experience teachers who had lower expectations for their learning and others to have higher expectations.

In fact, teacher expectations play an important role in students' learning.[28] Teachers who have high expectations believe that the students they teach will make accelerated growth, not simply "normal" progress. Teachers with lower expectations assign tasks that are less cognitively demanding, spend time repeating information over and over again, focus on classroom rules and procedures rather than learning, and accept a lower standard of work.

Learning to analyze the standards—which we will also discuss in this module—helps teachers understand the expectation for the grade level and content they teach. And when teachers do so in the presence of their peers, they are much more likely to consider the ways in which they can ensure students access the grade-level expectations. When teachers deeply understand the standards, including the skills and concepts contained within the standards, they can design learning experiences and evidence collection systems to monitor students' progress toward the learning goals.

Consequently, the story behind this question allows teachers to deeply understand the curriculum expectations and standards and thus internalize the expectations articulated in these documents. Although many school systems have adopted high-quality instructional materials (HQIMs) that are designed to provide a scope-and-sequence that is evidence-based and standards-aligned, the research[29] suggests that teachers spend a significant amount of time mixing and matching instructional materials. In fact, teachers spend about seven hours per week searching for materials and an additional five hours per week creating their own content.[30] If these are aligned with grade-level expectations, the time might be well spent, but "the caliber, rigor, and any rational sequencing of that material both within and across grade levels becomes a matter of luck and chance."[31] In contrast, when teachers and teams deeply understand the standards, they are more able to streamline their already adopted curriculum.

Video 1.3
Nancy discusses the ideas behind question 1
qrs.ly/m4ghob5

To ensure that students have access to HQIMs, teams need to be clear on the expectations for grade-level instruction of the standards, analyze those expectations, and then ensure that the materials they put in front of students meet the standards for quality. In districts that have formally adopted HQIMs, it is still important that teachers understand the standards so that they can interpret the evidence their students produce to determine when students have met the expectation or if the learners need additional supports to be successful.

NOTES

ANALYZING STANDARDS

Academic standards indicate what students should know and be able to do in each grade level and content area by the end of the school year. Academic standards are the result of negotiations in a community and are decided upon by policymakers. Educators analyze the standards to identify the specific concepts and skills students need to be taught, which leads to the identification of the learning progression: what comes first, what comes later, and what is taught toward the end of the unit. There are likely many logical learning progressions that will ensure students' success, and there may be some learning progressions that introduce concepts or skills for which students need more background knowledge. Developers of instructional materials also engage in this process. However, because they do not know the specific students in a given class, they may over- or under-shoot the learning progressions, which is why it is important for teams to develop or analyze the learning progressions based on their understanding of the standards and their students.

ASK A BOT

For inspiration, you can ask your AI system to provide you with options for learning progressions. Remember, there is not one right way to progress through the learning. Considering options can spark ideas for the team. You might use the following prompt:

> We are planning a unit for _____ grade, with the goal of helping students master these standards: [**LIST STANDARDS**]. Can you suggest two different ways to sequence the learning progression for this unit? Each sequence should take a different approach or route but still lead to students achieving the same learning goals.

A common way of analyzing standards is to focus on the concepts and skills contained within the standard. Generally speaking, the verbs and verb phrases describe the skills that students must develop, whereas the nouns and noun phrases identify the concepts that need to be learned.[32] This analysis helps teachers understand the type of thinking required or the depth of knowledge needed for students to be successful. For example, some standards focus on one idea, while others focus on several ideas. And still others focus on how ideas relate to one another or how ideas can be extended. Let's look at an example from fifth grade.

Standard	
Use place value understanding to round decimals to any place.	
Concepts (nouns):	**Skills (verbs):**
place value	use
decimals	round
place	

This simple analysis identifies the areas of content that students need to learn to be successful. As the teacher, you're on the lookout for students' understanding of these concepts and skills, which guides the development of instructional events and assessment opportunities.

As you probably noticed, the concepts (nouns) are fairly straightforward. But the skills (verbs) are a bit more complex. What does it mean to *use* when you are a fifth grader? How is that different from other grade standards that also use the word *use*? To maintain high expectations, teachers need to be clear about the skills students need to develop and the level of depth that is required by grade level. These make for great conversations with your colleagues.

There are several major cognitive moves that students must make to develop mastery of the standards (see Figure 1.1). Identifying the cognitive moves can help you and your team, but you still have to decide if you have high expectations for students in that particular grade level. Again, what does it mean to *use* at the fifth-grade level? As it turns out, that is a hard question to answer and one that plagues test makers. It's an estimation, not an exact science. But to ensure that students' learning leaps rather than lags, it's important to focus on the skills (verbs) and the depth of knowledge implied by the standard as a whole.

Figure 1.1 • Organization of Verbs in Standards

Add to: combine, deepen, improve, incorporate, integrate, introduce

Arrange: arrange, list, organize, sort

Big picture: comprehend, contextualize, orient, understand

(Continued)

(Continued)

Collaborate: contribute, engage, interact, participate, share

Compare: associate, categorize, classify, compare, connect, contrast, differentiate, discriminate, distinguish, link, match, relate

Create: accomplish, achieve, build, compose, construct, create, develop, draft, form, generate, initiate, produce, publish, record, stimulate

Decide: choose, decide, select

Define: define, delineate, determine, discern, establish, exemplify, identify, interpret, label, locate, name, recall, recognize

Elaborate: broaden, derive, elaborate, enhance, expand

Evaluate: assess, check, critique, evaluate, judge

Execute: advance, calculate, conduct, compute, employ, execute, navigate

Explain: answer, articulate, clarify, communicate, convey, describe, explain, express, inform, narrate, present, recount, report, respond, retell, state, summarize, synthesize

Hypothesize: anticipate, approximate, conjecture, consider, estimate, experiment, explore, hypothesize, pose, predict, test

Infer: conclude, deduce, generalize, infer, reason

Measure: gauge, measure, quantify

Metacognitive: appreciate, attend, design, monitor, persevere, plan, prepare, reflect, self-correct

Problem solve: figure out, overcome, problem solve, resolve, solve, surmount

Prove/argue: argue, assert, challenge, claim, confirm, defend, disagree, justify, persuade, promote, prove, quantify, specify, support, verify

Pull apart: analyze, decompose, decontextualize, diagnose, examine, grapple, investigate, partition, probe

Redo: redo, repeat, reread, revisit

Reference: acknowledge, cite, consult, plagiarize, refer, reference, trace

Seek information: acquire, ask, capture, compile, detect, elicit, encounter, evoke, find out, gather, listen, note, notice, observe, question, request, research, search, seek, study

Symbolize: act out, chart, conceptualize, demonstrate, depict, diagram, graph, illustrate, imagine, map, model, represent, symbolize, visualize

Transform: accentuate, adapt, adjust, alter, apply, conform, convert, edit, emphasize, manipulate, modify, paraphrase, rearrange, refine, replace, revise, rewrite, shape, shift, simplify, strengthen, substitute, tailor, transform, translate, update

Adapted from *Vocabulary for the Common Core*, pp. 57–88, by R. Marzano and J. Simms, Marzano Resources, 2013.

QUICK START

	I can start this tomorrow	I can begin this month	I need to discuss this with others	Resources needed
Identify the standards that apply to your grade level and content area(s).				
Review the standards for an upcoming series of lessons to identify the concepts (nouns) within the standard.				
Review the standards for an upcoming series of lessons to identify the skills (verbs) within the standards.				
Analyze the instructional materials for the alignment with agreed-upon vocabulary and definitions from the identified concepts and skills within the standards.				
Develop or analyze the learning progression such that there is a logical flow of learning.				
Analyze how the standards for your upcoming unit build on those from the previous grade level and connect to the next grade level. Identify gaps and overlaps.				

Available for download at https://companion.corwin.com/courses/PLC

IDENTIFYING LEARNING INTENTIONS

The standards identify what students need to know and be able to do at the end of the year. They represent the outcomes of the daily learning experiences that are designed and delivered. These learning intentions, learning goals, learning targets, or objectives are clear statements of the learning students will do on a given day in a given lesson.

Although teachers do not need to announce the learning objectives to students at the outset of the lesson, at some point during the learning process, students deserve to know what they are expected to learn. Learning intentions prime students about the learning to come and provide them an opportunity to reflect on their learning after the lesson. However, many teachers do not phrase the learning intention in a way that meets the true definition of the objective (which, we admit, is often written specifically for adults). Instead, teachers tend to introduce learning intentions with one of these general statements:

- I am learning [about, to, how, that . . .]
- We are learning [about, to, how, that . . .]

While these two statements convey to students the general topic or area of learning, they should be revised in such a way that they are accessible to students *while also maintaining the academic language of the standard*. In other words, learning intentions must be based on the analysis of the standards, and thus they must focus on the concepts and skills within the standards. Sample learning intentions include these statements:

- I am learning to generalize place value for multidigit whole numbers.
- I am learning how energy is transferred.
- I am learning about the ways authors introduce their ideas.

Each of these statements provides students an orientation to the learning experiences to come. Importantly, there is evidence that being clear about what students need to learn lessens the cognitive load on learners and increases their motivation to learn.[33]

QUICK START

	I can start this tomorrow	I can begin this month	I need to discuss this with others	Resources needed
Draft (or use a chatbot to draft) learning intentions.				
Sequence the learning intentions in a logical flow to develop students' skills and concepts.				
Revise the learning intentions for use next time based on students' response.				

Available for download at **https://companion.corwin.com/courses/PLC**

CRAFTING SUCCESS CRITERIA

Success is motivational; it makes us feel good. And success reinforces learning. Yes, we can and do learn from failure, but it's more rewarding to learn from success. Success criteria make the destination clear to students and allow them to monitor their progress toward the learning intention, seek feedback as they engage in learning tasks, and self-assess their performance as they learn. In addition, clear success criteria make students feel safer during the learning process as they understand what is expected of them and how they will know that they have learned something.[34]

For convenience, we start success criteria in one of two ways:

- I can . . .
- We can . . .

Of course, there are several ways to ensure that students know what success looks like, including rubrics, exemplars, modeling, and so on. Regardless of the format, the key is that students know what it means to have learned something. Ideally, there are several success criteria for each lesson. Even more ideal is an early win: Early in the lesson, students accomplish their first success criterion. In doing so, the reward pathway in their brain is fed neurotransmitters and feels good, thus encouraging learners to persist and obtain that same feeling again.

Let's say that a group of middle-school teachers agreed on the following learning intention: *I am learning about the way writers use figurative language*. The range of success criteria might include the following:

- I can identify the figurative language in a text.
- I can name the type of figurative language (e.g., simile, metaphor, alliteration, hyperbole, onomatopoeia, personification).
- I can explain what the figurative language means.
- I can identify the reason the author might have used the figurative language.
- I can use figurative language in my writing.

The first two statements are not really at the level of middle-school performance, but they are necessary prerequisites for achieving the others. Rapidly demonstrating success on the first two invites students to persist and figure out what the figurative language means. The last success criterion is beyond the expectations for middle school but seems like a logical extension for students as they begin to internalize an author's usage of this type of language.

ASK A BOT

Learning intentions and success criteria can be drafted by AI systems and then analyzed and improved by teacher teams. You might use the following frame to improve the quality of the output you receive from your chatbot:

I am a _____ grade teacher. We are focused on the following standard(s): [**INSERT STANDARDS**]. Develop learning intentions for ____ days in a logical flow so that my students develop their skills and concepts. Include the language of the standard and make the learning intentions accessible for my students. Based on this learning intention, [**INSERT LEARNING INTENTION**], develop _____ success criteria that include literal and conceptual understandings. Ensure that the language is accessible for my students. In the prompt, include the language of "I am learning . . ." for the learning intention and "I know that I have learned it when I can . . ." for the success criteria.

NOTES

QUICK START

	I can start this tomorrow	I can begin this month	I need to discuss this with others	Resources needed
Draft (or use a chatbot to draft) success criteria.				
Identify the types of evidence that need to be collected based on the success criteria.				
Revise the success criteria for use next time based on students' response.				

Available for download at **https://companion.corwin.com/courses/PLC**

TEACHER CLARITY PROTOCOL

Analyzing standards helps teams internalize the learning that their students need to do. Deep understanding of the standards helps with the selection of instructional materials and with the development of tasks, assignments, and assessments. With practice, engaging in this teacher clarity protocol requires less of a time investment.

Purpose: This protocol helps teams analyze standards and develop learning expectations for students. In some cases, teams analyze the content of instructional materials to determine if the objectives are appropriate for students or if they need to be revised using student-facing language. If the instructional materials do not have success criteria, then teams develop those as well.

STEP 1: Identify Standards for an Upcoming Learning Unit

- Based on a list of standards taught at specific times of the year, agree on the standards that will be the focus of the unit. If there is an approved pacing guide, use the standards appropriate for the upcoming unit.
- List the concepts and skills from the standards. You can use AI to assist.
- Organize the concepts and skills into a logical flow of ideas and information. You can use AI to assist.

STEP 2: Develop Learning Intentions

- Draft and agree upon at least one learning intention per day for the length of the unit of instruction. You can use AI to assist.

STEP 3: Develop Success Criteria

- Draft and agree upon at least one success criterion per learning intention that focuses on the content being learned. You can use AI to assist.
- Draft and agree upon at least one success criterion per learning intention that focuses on the linguistic demands of the lesson. Consider the vocabulary students need to learn, the language structures they need to use, or the language functions they need to develop. This success criterion typically involves language production—the speaking or writing students will do to demonstrate their understanding. You can use AI to assist.

STEP 4: Decide How the Learning Intentions and Success Criteria Will Be Shared With Students

- Discuss the range of ways that learning expectations can be shared with students. Are they posted or printed for students? Do students have self-assessment tools that include the learning intentions and success criteria?

STEP 5: Identify the Relevance and Value of the Learning

- Discuss the ways in which teachers can share the importance, relevance, or value of what students are expected to learn. Note that there are many ways to hook students and ensure that they see the value of their learning.

Quality Checklist for the Learning Intentions and Success Criteria

Learning Intentions[35]

- ☐ Learning intentions are visible and usable for students.

(Continued)

(Continued)

- ☐ Learning intentions are discussed throughout the lesson.
- ☐ Students are given time to reflect on, ask questions about, and discuss the learning intentions.
- ☐ Connections are made to the learning intentions while students are engaged in the learning.
- ☐ Students are asked to monitor their progress using the learning intentions.
- ☐ Learning intentions are directly connected to the standard(s).

Success Criteria[36]

- ☐ Success criteria are visible and usable for students.
- ☐ Success criteria are shared and clarified with students during the learning.
- ☐ Success criteria communicate *I will know I have learned it when I can . . .* with specific parts or steps needed for success.
- ☐ Success criteria include worked examples, exemplars, or models for clarity.
- ☐ Students are asked to use the success criteria to self-assess learning progress.
- ☐ Students are asked to provide feedback to peers using success criteria.
- ☐ Success criteria are used to provide feedback to students.
- ☐ Each criterion for success moves the students incrementally closer to the learning intention.

Video 1.4
A team works through the Teacher Clarity protocol
qrs.ly/ezghob7

NOTES

TABLE OF SPECIFICATIONS

Typically, standards are not taught one at a time. Instead, they are bundled into units of instruction that last several weeks. It is often more efficient for teams to plan at the unit level with many standards taught so that they can devote other team meeting times to other PLC+ questions. One way to consider the ways that standards fit together is through the development of a table of specifications.[37]

A table of specifications is a more sophisticated way of analyzing standards to identify the knowledge and skills required. The table includes the academic terminology required of the standard, as well as the facts, rules, principles, processes, and procedures. These are usually found in the concepts from the standards. In addition, the table of specifications includes the translation or transfer skills, application, and analysis or synthesis required, which are generally found in the skills of the standards. Once done, teams can use the table of specification to accomplish the following:

- Identify the amount of instructional time required to develop students' understanding of each aspect of the standards.

- Ensure that the confirmative assessment used to document students' learning is inclusive of all aspects of the standard.

Figure 1.2 provides a sample table of specifications for a world history class. Notice the unit goals that align with the standards and then the various aspects of the standards that students would need to learn to reach proficiency.

Figure 1.2 • Table of Specifications for Modern World History: Unit 2—Connecting Hemispheres

Unit Goals	Knowledge of . . .				Skills for . . .		
	Terms	Facts	Concepts & Principles	Processes & Procedures	Translation or Transfer	Application	Analysis & Synthesis
I can explain the development and influence of the Silk Road and Indian Ocean trade routes.	Silk Road, Indian Ocean trade	Trade routes connected Asia, Africa, and Europe.	Trade promotes cultural diffusion and political influence.	Analyze maps and primary sources to identify trade routes and goods.	Describe the cultural and political influence along trade routes.	Map trade routes and assess their impact on civilizations.	
I can analyze how trade influenced the development of African empires.	Ghana, Mali, Songhai, caravan, diffusion	African empires grew through trade networks and developed cultural identities.	Trade networks contributed to economic and cultural growth in African empires.		Explain the connection between trade and empire expansion.	Assess the role of trade in the rise of African empires.	Compare the political, social, and economic effects of trade on African empires.

(Continued)

(Continued)

Unit Goals	Knowledge of . . .				Skills for . . .		
	Terms	Facts	Concepts & Principles	Processes & Procedures	Translation or Transfer	Application	Analysis & Synthesis
I can explain how the Black Death acted as a catalyst for social, political, and economic change in Europe.	Black Death, Catholic Church, feudalism	The Black Death weakened feudalism and Church authority in Europe.	Disease spread along trade routes; led to social and political shifts.	Categorize effects of the Black Death by social, political, and economic impact.	Describe the impact of the Black Death on medieval society.		Analyze and synthesize the long-term social, economic, and political impacts of the Black Death.
I can describe the causes and effects of the Italian and Northern Renaissance.	Humanism, secularism, individualism	Renaissance ideas challenged Church authority and promoted individualism.	Humanism encouraged secularism and questioning of authority.		Distinguish between Italian and Northern Renaissance characteristics.	Compare the influence of Renaissance figures on European thought.	Analyze Renaissance texts and artworks to understand their cultural impact.
I can identify the main motivations for European exploration and the effects of the Columbian Exchange.	Columbian Exchange, mercantilism, Zheng He	The Columbian Exchange spread goods, diseases, and ideas globally.	Exploration affected indigenous populations and European economies.	Analyze explorers' contributions, and motivations; complete T-chart on mercantilist policies.	Describe items exchanged and their impacts on the Old and New Worlds.		Analyze the positive and negative effects of exploration on indigenous and European societies.
I can analyze the causes and consequences of the Atlantic Slave Trade.	Atlantic Slave Trade, colonization	Colonization and labor demand in the Americas expanded the African slave trade.	Trade and colonization drove the growth of slavery as an economic system.	Study data and primary sources on slave trade routes and impacts.	Summarize social and economic effects of the Atlantic Slave Trade.	Develop an infographic on causes and effects of the slave trade.	Analyze economic motivations and social consequences of the Atlantic Slave Trade across regions.
I can construct an argument on the consequences of increased global connections and interactions.	Debate, evidence	Global interactions led to significant cultural, economic, and social changes.	Increased interaction has both positive and negative consequences.	Synthesize research on global interactions' influence on civilizations.	Identify key arguments for and against global interactions.	Develop and support a position in a debate on global interactions.	Construct a well-supported argument analyzing long-term consequences of global connections.

ASK A BOT

PLC+ teams can use AI systems to draft a table of specifications for the team to analyze and improve. You might use the following frame to improve the quality of the output you receive from your chatbot:

> Using the attached document as a model [**UPLOAD A DOCUMENT**], develop a table of specifications for students in _____ grade based on the following standards: [**INSERT STANDARDS**]. Make sure to include the following categories: terms; facts, rules, and principles; processes and procedures; transfer skills or translation; application; and analysis and synthesis.

Note that creating a table of specifications is a bit more complex than identifying learning intentions and success criteria, so you may have to engage in a dialogue with your chatbot to make incremental improvements in the output.

NOTES

QUICK START

	I can start this tomorrow	I can begin this month	I need to discuss this with others	Resources needed
Identify the standards that can be combined into a learning unit or that are commonly taught together in your HQIMs.				
Identify, or use a chatbot to identify, the "knowledge of" categories.				
Identify, or use a chatbot to identify, the "skills for" categories.				
Analyze the table of specifications for its alignment with the concepts and skills within the standards.				
Consider all aspects of the table of specifications for lesson design and assessment development.				

Available for download at **https://companion.corwin.com/courses/PLC**

CASE IN POINT: A QUESTION OF SUCCESS

The second-grade teachers at Green Valley Elementary School met to analyze standards and identify learning intentions and success criteria. They found the process of naming the concepts and skills relatively easy, but it was much harder to agree on what the verb meant for their students. One of the standards that they focused on read as follows: *Estimate lengths using units of inches, feet, centimeters, and meters.*

As the discussion began, one of the teachers, Brandi Weston, said, "I'm not sure that I ever really paid attention to the word *estimate* like this. I mean, we teach them the measurement systems, but how close do their estimates need to be to be an estimate?"

One of her colleagues, Marco Jimenez, agreed, adding, "I wonder how far off their estimates would be. I think with some practice they could get pretty good at this. But I don't have an answer to how close they need to be for the estimate to be considered good enough. I think we should make this part of the lessons when we focus on measuring, especially when they measure to determine how much longer one object is compared with another."

Ms. Weston responded, "I agree with you that we could add the estimating into each lesson and into some practice work for students and their families so that we can see what we still need to teach them. Maybe we should include success criteria on this one to our lessons, such as, *I can explain my thinking when I estimate lengths.* This way, we can have the students tell us what they were thinking so that we can figure out what they still need to learn."

What's Your Advice?

- How can teams determine the rigor or expectation of the skills included in the standards?

- How might they collect information about what their students can already do in terms of the skill of estimating?

- Is the success criterion proposed by Ms. Weston useful and appropriate? Why or why not?

Video 1.5
An activator reflects on the case in point
qrs.ly/ckghob9

Module 1: Where Are We Going? 69

CROSSCUTTING VALUES CHECK

How is access to grade-level standards enacted at your school? Is it access for all or just for some? Consider these reflective questions to spark discussion with colleagues.

Equity and Fairness

- What steps have we taken to understand our own biases and perceptions?
- Do we recognize the historical barriers some students face in their learning journey?
- Do we understand the power of our collective decisions to address fairness for all students?

High Expectations

- Do we believe that all students can learn and achieve at high levels, and do we introduce them all to the appropriate grade-level standards?
- Do we believe that all of our students can achieve success?
- Do our learning intentions and success criteria reflect rigorous learning expectations for students?
- Would the students furthest from success agree that we hold high expectations for them and believe they can achieve success?

Individual and Collective Efficacy

- Do our skills in analyzing standards grow and develop as we work together as a team?
- Do we set goals for our time together and believe that we can accomplish our goals?
- Do we have evidence that our efforts are impacting our learning and the learning of our students?

Activators

- Do we develop and foster relational trust?
- Do we regularly prioritize time across the year to develop and foster relationships and trust with and between students?
- Do we have protocols for collaboratively analyzing standards and developing learning intentions and success criteria?
- Do we willingly share ideas but not try to sell our ideas to others?

SELF-ASSESSMENT

The question "Where are we going?" focuses attention on the intentions for learning. It challenges us to move beyond pacing guides and curriculum maps to make clear-eyed decisions about the learning path we will blaze. As you pursue answers to this question, make sure to keep the end in mind: What is it that we want our learners to know, understand, and be able to do?

Rapid Assessment:

We define our expectations through learning intentions and success criteria, and these definitions involve learning progressions over time, moving to the point of equity of access and opportunity for learning for all students.

1	2	3	4	5
Not Begun or Not Initiated	Very Limited Evidence of Capacity	Some Evidence of Capacity	Evidence of Capacity and Limited Evidence of Effective Implementation	Evidence of Capacity and Demonstrated Effective Implementation

Queries for Conducting a Detailed Assessment:

	Where Are We Going?	Not Begun or Not Initiated	Very Limited Evidence of Capacity	Some Evidence of Capacity	Evidence of Capacity and Limited Evidence of Effective Implementation	Evidence of Capacity and Demonstrated Effective Implementation
1.1	We regularly analyze expectations based upon the standards and/or curriculum that guide our efforts.	1	2	3	4	5
1.2	Our efforts result in equity of access for all learners.	1	2	3	4	5
1.3	Our efforts result in opportunity for learning for all learners.	1	2	3	4	5
1.4	We regularly outline learning progressions.	1	2	3	4	5
1.5	Our efforts reflect true learning progressions over time, rather than a given lesson at a specific point or points in time.	1	2	3	4	5
1.6	We present instruction that includes explicit success criteria that our students understand.	1	2	3	4	5
1.7	We present instruction that includes explicit learning intentions that our students understand.	1	2	3	4	5

 Available for download at **https://companion.corwin.com/courses/PLC**

NOTICE AND REFLECT

ESSENTIAL QUESTION

How can teacher teams identify the learning journeys of their students?

THINK ABOUT

- How do the academic content standards impact planning decisions?
- How are our expectations for students' learning telegraphed based on what we believe they can learn?
- How do we maintain high expectations, even when students have unfinished learning that impacts their performance?

START – STOP – KEEP

Based on what you learned in this module, answer the questions below.

Start: What practice(s) would you like to start doing?

Stop: What practice(s) would you like to stop doing?

Keep: What practice(s) would you like to keep doing?

NOTES

WHERE ARE WE NOW?

2 WHERE ARE WE NOW?

As humans, we are in a continual state of revising what we know and can do. We build our skills and knowledge, revising our understanding of the world and going from the known to the new. As educators, when we activate and build our students' background knowledge, we acknowledge this reality, and this approach results in better outcomes for the learners.[38] As David Ausubel noted, "The most important single factor influencing learning is what the learner already knows. Ascertain this and teach [the learner] accordingly."[39]

Students are not blank slates as they enter our classrooms. They have experiences, gifts, talents, strengths, assets, and funds of knowledge. Wise educators recognize what students already know and draw upon students' assets as a strategy to increase student efficacy and belonging as they work to extend their knowledge. Effective educators also recognize that they may need to build students' background knowledge when they have unfinished learning.

Importantly, as our colleague John Almarode reminds us, there is a difference between things that students *need to know* versus things that are *neat to know*. Not all the content from previous lessons is critical for the learning right now, but some of that knowledge is likely vital for the learners' success. And really, there is no bad place to be on the continuum of a learning journey. Yes, we want more for our students and we work to accelerate their learning, but if we think of their unfinished learning as a deficit, then we run the risk of lowering our expectations. Then our logic becomes, "They don't know this, and they don't know that, so how can they learn the content for this year?"

Effective teaching and learning exist in the gap between what students already know and can do and what they need to know and be able to do. Unless we have this information about our students, we will struggle to plan meaningful learning experiences for them. Consequently, it's important for teams to collect and analyze evidence to identify students' strengths and then compare those data with the expected learning outcomes.

Essential Question

HOW DOES KNOWING STUDENTS' CURRENT PERFORMANCE SUPPORT THEIR LEARNING JOURNEY?

Video 2.1
An elementary team discusses question 2
qrs.ly/hgghoba

Video 2.2
A secondary team discusses question 2
qrs.ly/vmghobb

NOTES

TWO TRUTHS AND A LIE

Two of these statements are true; one is false. Can you spot the lie?

1. A significant percentage of instructional minutes are devoted to content students already know.

2. Strengths-based approaches acknowledge the future learning needs of students.

3. Some students are fast learners, and some are slow learners.

It is true that, on average, a significant percentage of instructional minutes are devoted to content students have already mastered. In fact, some estimates suggest that between 40 and 50 percent of instructional time is squandered on content students already know.[40] Unfortunately, it's rare for all the students to have the same background knowledge and to have mastered the same content. Thus, teams need to assess these factors so that they can extend the learning of all students.

The second statement is also true. Strengths-based approaches focus on building from the strengths to address next-steps learning. In analyzing a student's strengths, teachers and teams identify what the student can accomplish with educational support, often referred to as the zone of proximal development. This approach frames the conversation about teacher expectations by focusing on the potential for growth and the role of support in helping students reach their next level of learning.

Thus, the lie? It's about fast and slow learners. The evidence clearly indicates that we all generally learn at the same rate. In a study of 1.3 million student interactions from different kinds of educational technologies, it became clear that learners master new concepts by having opportunities to practice them.[41] Some students have had more exposures and thus need less instruction or fewer opportunities to practice. It's really about the head start that some students have rather than the speed at which we acquire knowledge and skills. Other students have not had the same number of exposures as their classmates. After all, it is hard to learn what you haven't been taught. And that's the power of asking "Where are we now?"—recognizing where students are in their learning journey.

Module 2: Where Are We Now?

THE STORY BEHIND THE QUESTION (WHERE ARE WE NOW?)

Two factors influenced our decision to include this question in the PLC+ framework. The first is the impact of deficit thinking.[42] When we have a deficit mindset, we tend to focus on problems rather than on potential, and we rationalize lowered expectations because of the focus on the gaps in current performance levels. In fact, a deficit mindset can lead educators to do the following:

- Blame students for their disadvantages
- Expect less from students
- Provide less help to students
- Ignore students' cultural and community strengths
- Diminish the value of students' lived experiences

In contrast, when we see students for the gifts and strengths they possess, the opposite becomes true. We raise expectations, boost students' sense of efficacy and agency, increase student belonging, and support students in their learning journeys.

Our jobs involve building on students' strengths to help them develop learned talent. As Adam Grant notes, "If natural talent determines where people start, learned talent or character affects how far they go."[43] Although we have little impact on students' natural talent, we have a profound impact on learned talent, which includes perseverance, passions, and prosocial skills that students acquire through daily interactions with others.

The second factor that influenced our decision to include the question "Where are we now?" was the unintended consequences of key standards, essential standards, highly tested standards, and so on that result in some students not being taught all the content articulated in the standards. We have not supported the efforts to cherry-pick some standards and not others because students deserve to learn all the standards expected of them. If not, performance gaps persist and can be exacerbated. We acknowledge that there were an awful lot of standards in some places for students to learn, which led to the belief that standards in the US were a mile wide and an inch deep. But that has changed as the world focused on fewer but deeper standards.

The essential or priority standards are "a carefully selected subset of the total list of the grade-specific and course-specific standards within each content area that students must know and be able to do by the end of the school year in order to be prepared for the standards at the next grade level or course."[44] These priority standards compare with supporting standards, which are standards that enhance the priority standards but do not receive the same amount of focused instruction and assessment. According to some authorities, priority standards should meet the following selection criteria.[45]

- ***Endurance:*** Knowledge and skills of value beyond a single test date. Will the standard be employed exactly as it is in life beyond the school walls? Does it represent how things are really done?

- ***Leverage:*** Knowledge and skills of value in multiple disciplines. Is the standard transferable and even necessary for learners to access skills and content in other areas or fields?

- ***Readiness:*** Knowledge and skills necessary for success in the next grade level, the next instruction level, or the state test. Is the standard a building block that other standards are contingent on?

Source: Kramer, S. (2015). *How to Leverage PLCs for School Improvement.* Solution Tree.

Imagine the lack of cohesion if teams followed a recommended protocol that identified "seven to twelve or approximately one-third of state standards" to teach.[46] As this process describes it, individual teachers decide on essential standards, talk about their selections with their colleagues, check with testing information and other grade levels or courses, and then use those standards as their curriculum. The experiences in one school could be widely different from those in another school, and the impact on learners could be profoundly negative. What if the team guesses wrong?

When teachers and teams focus on the grade-level expectations and intentionally develop students' skills and knowledge aligned with those standards, learning accelerates.[47,48] High-performing schools teach all the standards. However, some standards require more time than others and deserve more instructional focus.

Thus, the evidence and our experience suggest that teams need to identify what students already know—that is, to consider "Where are we now?"—so that they can reduce the number of instructional minutes that are redundant, allowing them more time to develop students' proficiency on all the standards. Anything less than that approach results in lowered expectations for some students and contributes negatively to the variance within a school.

Video 2.3
Doug discusses the story behind question 2
qrs.ly/h8ghobe

NOTES

INITIAL ASSESSMENTS

Collecting evidence about what students already know and can do helps teachers identify student strengths, reduces the amount of time spent on concepts and skills students have already mastered, and allows for greater customization of the learning journey for students. Holding high expectations for all students requires not only knowing what they know and focusing on the same success criteria for all students but also designing the learning experiences to meet students' individual needs.

Initial assessments come in a variety for formats, such as these:

- Writing samples and other samples of student work
- Interviews and observations of students
- Checklists or rubrics of skills or behaviors
- Quizzes
- Self-assessment

The following key words describe what effective initial assessment should be like:[49]

- **Fair.** All individuals are treated equally, and there should be no discrimination, even implicitly.
- **Positive.** The initial assessment experience should be positive for learners, and it should keep stress to a minimum.
- **Consistent.** Consistency will help the team feel confident that the results of initial assessment are right the first time and every time.
- **Rigorous.** It is equally important that the results of initial assessment are sound and provide a true picture of the learners' skills, knowledge, and learning needs.

- **Documented**. The system should generate records that are simple to use and understand.
- **Linked**. The assessment should be linked to a dynamic learning plan that informs each individual's development and is continually reviewed and updated.

It's important to highlight these indicators, especially the positive experience. Students should not feel shame because they don't yet know the content. Instead, as teachers, we need to remind them that they are learning this new material and explain that these initial assessments help us develop better learning experiences for them. The assessments are not graded or sent home; they are analyzed for next-steps learning.

Consider the following questions as you develop an initial assessment to identify what students already know.

Considerations	Your Response
What do I already know about my students from previous units of instruction?	
What type(s) of assessment items will help me identify areas of prior learning? [ ] Writing sample [ ] Observation or interview [ ] Knowledge inventory [ ] Checklist or rubric [ ] Other	How will I collect this information?
How can I ensure that my initial assessments are free from bias?	

ASK A BOT

Most AI systems are reasonably good at generating a list of concepts and skills required for a unit of learning. From this list, your team can create a quick tool to identify what students already know and still need to know. You may use a prompt like this:

> We are teaching the following concepts and skills to students in _____ grade: [**LIST SKILLS AND CONCEPTS FROM THE STANDARD(S)**]. We need to assess what they have already learned about this so that we don't unintentionally teach the same things. Generate a list of at least fifteen items that we can use to assess students' background knowledge.

QUICK START

	I can start this tomorrow	I can begin this month	I need to discuss this with others	Resources needed
Collect initial assessment information from students that is fair, consistent, and rigorous.				
Make the initial assessment experience a positive experience for students.				
Review the standards for an upcoming series of lessons to identify the skills (verbs) within the standards.				
Use the initial assessment information to plan instructional experiences for students.				
Use the initial assessment evidence in conversations about students' learning journeys.				
Reflect on the assumption that some students are "fast" learners while others are "slow" learners. Instead, consider how differences in prior exposure and learning opportunities influence the pace at which students grasp new concepts.				

Available for download at **https://companion.corwin.com/courses/PLC**

FOCUSING ON STRENGTHS

Strengths-based education has been around for decades, but education tends to revert to gaps and deficits when we talk about students and their learning. Generally speaking, our profession is much more akin to medicine in which the doctor attempts to quickly diagnose and treat a patient rather than to focus on what the person is doing well and what aspects of their health are strong. In doing so, we tend to focus on unfinished learning rather than on strengths. However, we know from the research evidence that "a strengths-based approach can help build student confidence, encourage efficacious behaviors, and support life-long learning pursuits."[50]

Importantly, a strengths-based approach begins with what students can presently do *and* what they will be able to do with educational supports. The design of those educational supports flows from knowing what it is that students can already do. Figure 2.1 provides a general summary of a strengths-based approach.

Figure 2.1 • Summary of a Strengths-Based Approach

	A Strengths-Based Approach
IS	• valuing everyone equally and focusing on what the child can do rather than what the child cannot do • describing learning and development respectfully and honestly • building on a child's abilities within their zones of proximal and potential development • acknowledging that people experience difficulties and challenges that need attention and support • identifying what is taking place when learning and development go well, so that it may be reproduced, further developed, and strengthened

A Strengths-Based Approach	
IS NOT	- only about "positive" things - a way of avoiding the truth - about accommodating bad behaviour - fixated on problems - about minimizing concerns - one-sided - a tool to label individuals

Source: Victoria Department of Education and Early Childhood Development. (2012). *Strength-based approach: A guide to writing transition and learning and development statements* (p. 9).

In addition to changing our mindsets about deficits versus strengths, as teachers we need effective tools to uncover the sometimes-hidden strengths our students possess. We can do this in multiple ways, including the following:

- **Observations**. Pay close attention to how your students interact, solve problems, and express themselves. Look for patterns in their behavior and achievements.
- **Information from others**. Solicit input from other teachers, parents/guardians, and peers about each student's strengths.
- **Student reflections**. Encourage students to reflect on their own strengths through journals or discussion prompts.
- **Student interviews or surveys**. Invite students as a focus group to your PLC+ team meeting to ask them about their learning, or provide them with an anonymous survey link to offer their perspectives.
- **Work samples**. Analyze students' work across different subjects to identify areas where they excel.

It is important to note that a strengths-based approach does not prevent educators from focusing on what students still need to learn. In fact, teachers can pair the strength with the next step in learning, as is the case with "if/then" statements such as these:

- If students have demonstrated success with spelling consonant-vowel-consonant words, then they can start learning how to blend consonants together, such as *snap, snow*, and *snug*.
- If students can consistently add fractions with conceptual understanding, then they are ready to start multiplying fractions.
- If students have experienced success with finding evidence in the text, then they are ready to identify the claims.
- If students can demonstrate understanding of the rock cycle, then they are ready to identify different rock types to interpret the geological history of a location.

These statements clearly recognize students' strengths and then focus on the next step of the learning journey. By taking this approach, educators build on students' strengths, making connections with the concepts and skills students have already learned.

Whenever we create tools for collecting and analyzing student assessment information, we should focus on their strengths and construct the tools accordingly. For example, many rubrics are focused on what the student cannot do (such as "The student is not able to add single-digit numbers") or include language such as *does not meet standard* or *needs improvement*. What if, instead, the rubrics, checklists, and inventories were focused on what the student *could* do, as is the case in the sample rubric in Figure 2.2?

Figure 2.2 • Math Assessment Rubric

Assessment Task	The student correctly does the following:	Evidence, Feedback, and Notes
Items 1–4	Explains what an imaginary number is and can contrast it with real numbers	
Items 5–8	Reduces imaginary numbers to their simplest radical form	
Rich task	Cites at least two applications for imaginary numbers	
Interview	Understands the relationship between Cartesian, polar, and exponential forms (Euler's formula) of representation for imaginary numbers	

When the tools invite a focus on strengths, teachers and their teams are much more likely to begin discussions on student assets. In doing so, they recognize strengths and reduce the amount of time spent on skills and concepts students already know. And, as an added benefit, teachers see their students in a positive light and recognize the impact that they and their colleagues have had on students' learning journeys.

ASK A BOT

You can be on the lookout for strengths by asking a chatbot to review the content of lessons and identify a range of strengths that students might exhibit as part of the learning process. You can use this sample prompt:

> Based on the following lessons/standards/learning intentions [**INSERT THEM HERE**] for students in grade _____, what would be five strengths that students could exhibit? Include strengths that are concepts and skills. List the strengths in student-facing language.

QUICK START

	I can start this tomorrow	I can begin this month	I need to discuss this with others	Resources needed
Analyze student assessments to identify strengths and skills.				
Focus our team conversations on strengths first.				
Develop tools that highlight what students can do.				
Link strengths to next steps for learning.				

Available for download at **https://companion.corwin.com/courses/PLC**

INCLUDING FOCAL STUDENTS

To help increase the number of students who benefit from our existing and future practices, PLC+ teams can foster learning partnerships with a representative group of students. This partnership also benefits members of the PLC+ team by guiding educators to new approaches that can benefit all the students in their care. Specifically, it requires the team to learn about who the students are, how they think, how they learn, and what perceptions they have of the classroom and school. The inclusion of focal students allows you to monitor learners' progress and seek their feedback regarding the investigation cycle you and your PLC+ team are embarking upon. It also supports the focal students as they utilize their assets and strengths and work with the team to achieve goals.[51]

We encourage teams to select three to five students per member to gauge progress and monitor the investigation. In doing so, the learners become a key part of the investigation itself and can inform the team's actions throughout. The National Equity Project recommends teams consider the following criteria to guide selection of focal students:[52]

- Students we can learn from
- Students who are not showing adequate progress toward grade level standards and who are unlikely to experience academic success as they move through future grade levels
- Students who are outside the sphere of success[53] or currently not being fully served by our school
- Students whose school attendance is consistent enough to be able to track progress and follow up on intervention efforts
- Students who are often representative of a larger group of students with similar skill-gap challenges

The questions you ask and tasks you design for focal students should align with the specific focus of your PLC+ team's investigation cycle. For example, if a PLC+ team is exploring how to improve student engagement during collaborative group work, then the team might select a diverse group of focal students who are quieter participants, who actively avoid group activities, or who struggle to contribute during group activities.

PLC members could engage these students in conversations with questions such as these:

- What do you enjoy most about working in groups?
- What challenges do you face when working with peers?
- What is your favorite type of group work?
- What could your teacher or classmates do to make group work more meaningful for you?

Then, based on insights gathered from observations during group work and these discussions, PLC members might adjust group work strategies. As a further step, they could invite focal students to reflect on the changes, asking questions like these:

- Did you notice any changes in group work this week?
- What made the task easier or harder for you?

ASK A BOT

Consider asking this AI prompt to allow you to get targeted recommendations on the types of questions you could ask focal students to get meaningful feedback that is connected to the goals of the PLC investigative cycle:

> My PLC+ team is focused on **[INSERT SPECIFIC FOCUS OF THE INVESTIGATION CYCLE]**. I want to design effective questions for students that align with this focus. What types of questions should I ask to gain insights into their experiences, challenges, and successes related to this area of learning? Also, please provide examples of questions that would help uncover useful observations and actionable insights to refine our teaching practice.

By focusing on a small, diverse group of students, PLC+ teams can identify patterns in learning, pinpoint specific barriers, and gather actionable data to adjust their practices. These focal students serve as a representation of the broader classroom population, ensuring that any intervention is equitable and responsive to varying needs. Additionally, monitoring focal students helps teams stay focused and purposeful, fostering deeper discussions about teaching and learning outcomes.

Not only do focal students serve as a means for the PLC+ team to learn with, from, and alongside, but they also allow you to respond in real time to adjust or refine existing approaches and to try different approaches throughout the investigation cycle. In the process, they can provide insight to help the team understand which approaches have a powerful impact and then apply those learnings to larger groups of students (see Figure 2.3). PLC+ teams can also include focal students in some of your team meetings so they can offer feedback and give the team an opportunity to ask them questions. Some of our very best meetings have been conducted with focal students serving as team members throughout the investigation cycle. Importantly, this approach serves as a reminder that we design "with" not "for" students.[54]

Figure 2.3 • Why Focal Students?

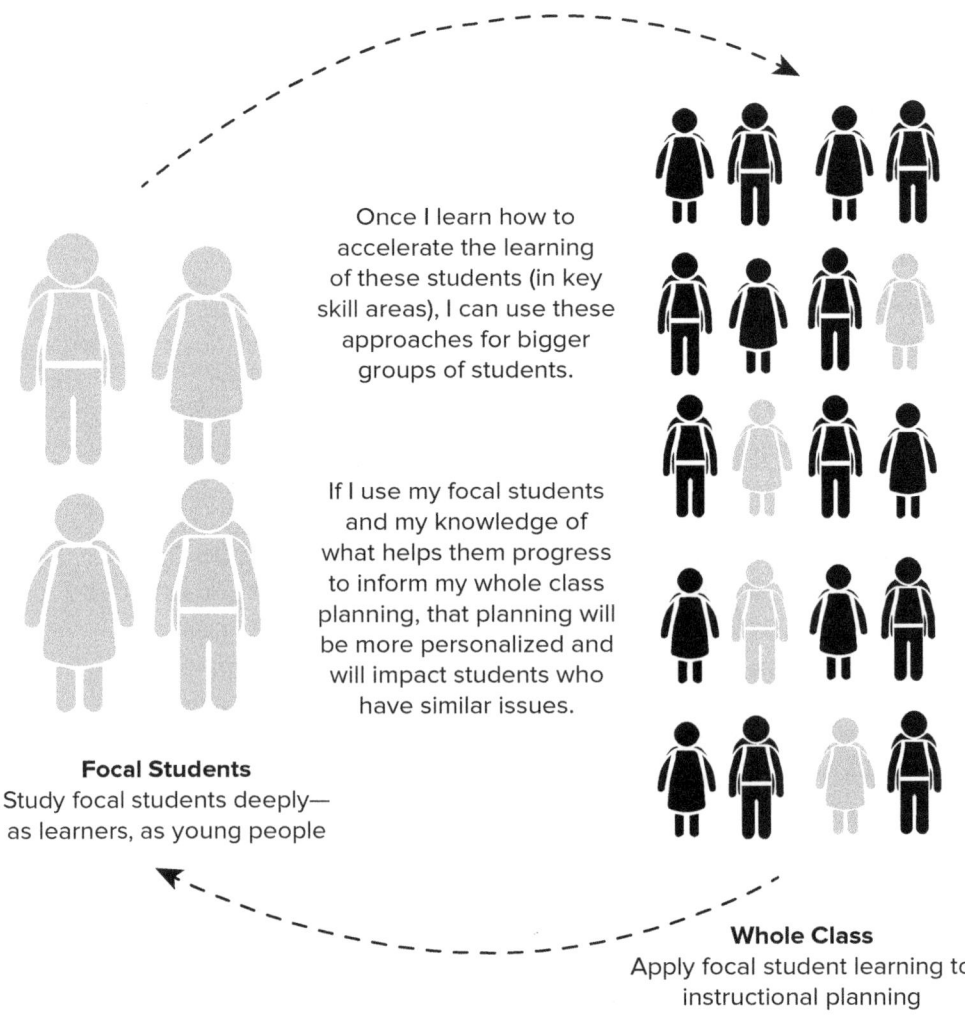

Source: Why Focal Students, National Equity Project[55]

QUICK START

	I can start this tomorrow	I can begin this month	I need to discuss this with others	Resources needed
Choose three to five focal students per team member. Ensure the selection includes diverse perspectives to maximize impact.				
Identify focal students based on the unique assets and strengths they bring to the classroom. Consider providing activities and opportunities for students to explore their strengths. Opportunities could also include chances for students to reflect on their strengths related to a specific task or assignment.				
Include plans to collect feedback from focal students about their experiences with the interventions.				
Consider a broad array of influences, including academic, social, and community factors.				
Track multiple data points for each focal student. Go beyond academic performance by monitoring behavioral, social-emotional, and engagement-related data.				

Available for download at **https://companion.corwin.com/courses/PLC**

DATA ANALYSIS PROTOCOL

Teams need tools to discuss the data they collect. Protocols help keep team members focused and moving through a process to make decisions. Without clear protocols, teams can be sidetracked or focus on factors they cannot change. There is a difference between our sphere of concern and our sphere of influence. Data protocols help teams recognize their concerns and then focus their efforts on aspects of the data they can influence.

Purpose: This protocol draws from the Liberatory Design approach to support PLC+ teams as they examine data. By focusing on empathy, situational awareness, and reflection, teams seek to understand both the stories behind the data and the broader context that shapes student experiences. This approach encourages a meaningful, student-centered analysis that respects diverse perspectives and considers systemic factors.

Suggested Time: 40 minutes

Preparation for Data Analysis

- **Materials Needed**: Copies of data, highlighters, chart paper, note-taking guides
- **Roles**: Activator (to guide the process), Recorder (to document key insights), and Timekeeper
- **Activator Preparation**: Begin with a reminder of the importance of empathy, noticing, and reflection in the process.

STEP 1: Empathize: Begin With Student Experiences (10 minutes)

- **Notice and Reflect: Silent Reflection (3 minutes)**

  Each team member reviews the quantitative and qualitative data, noting initial reactions with a focus on the students behind the numbers and descriptions.

- **Guiding Questions for Silent Reflection**:
  - What student stories might the data be reflecting?
  - Who might be experiencing success, and who might be struggling based on these patterns?

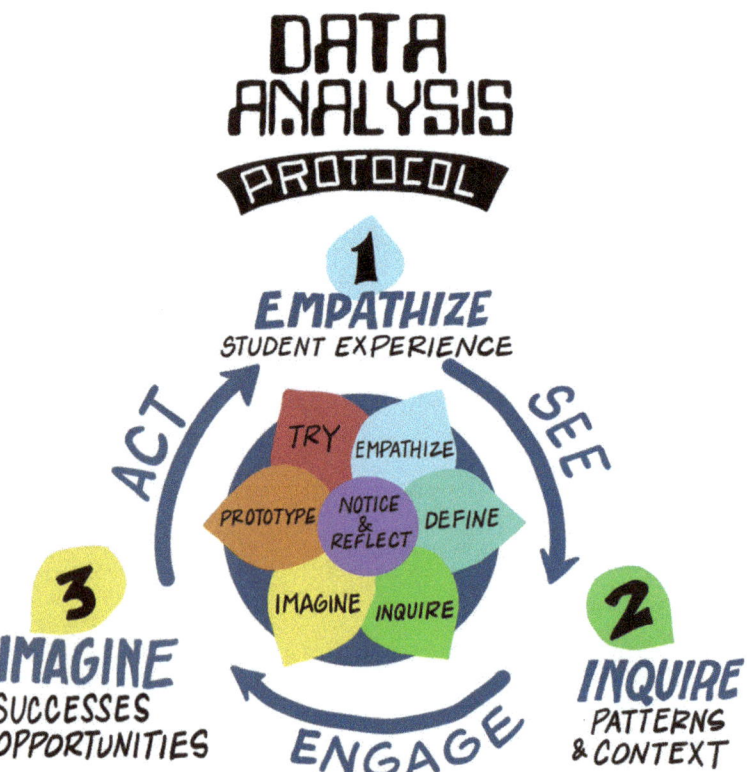

Adapted from "Liberatory Design for Equity" by the National Equity Project. Derived from Anaissie, T., Cary, V., Clifford, D., Malarkey, T. & Wise, S. (2021). Liberatory Design. www.liberatorydesign.com.

- **Group Discussion (7 minutes)**

  Share reflections, focusing on understanding student experiences as well as teacher experiences.
  - **Sample Dialogue Prompts:**
  - What do we imagine a student's day looks like based on the data?
  - What might students feel or think about their learning experiences here?
    - Document insights on a chart to visualize perspectives.

Step 2: See the System: Identify Patterns and Context (10 minutes)

- **Individual Observations (3 minutes)**
  - Note any patterns, surprises, or contextual factors that stand out. Consider cultural, social, and systemic influences that might impact the data.
  - **Group Discussion (7 minutes)**
  - **Guiding Questions:**
    - What patterns or gaps do we observe?
    - What environmental or systemic factors might be contributing to these results?
  - **Document Findings:** Record patterns and contextual observations, ensuring perspectives are inclusive and reflective of diverse student experiences.

Step 3: Imagine: Reflect on Successes and Opportunities for Growth (10 minutes)

- **Identifying Strengths (5 minutes)**
  - **Guiding Questions:**
    - What positive outcomes do we see, and what strengths can we build on?
    - Where might students be experiencing success in their learning?
- **Exploring Challenges (5 minutes)**
  - **Guiding Questions:**
    - What challenges do these data reveal?
    - How can we view these challenges as opportunities for growth and transformation?
- Summarize both strengths and areas for growth, emphasizing collective sense making and shared learning.

Step 4: Take Action to Learn: Synthesize Key Insights and Reflect on Next Steps (10 minutes)

- **Synthesis (5 minutes)**

  The group identifies two to three key insights from the data, focusing on actionable and equitable steps.
  - **Questions for Reflection:**
    - How do these insights inform our approach to creating a supportive learning environment?
    - What adjustments could we make to better meet all students' needs?
    - How will we narrow the disparities between groups of learners?
- **Notice and Reflect: Reflect on the Protocol (5 minutes)**
    - Discuss how the analysis process felt and any insights about the team's collaborative approach.
    - **Plus/Delta:** Identify strengths in the process and potential improvements for future sessions, fostering a mindset of continuous growth.

Quality Checklist for Data Analysis

- ☐ Student strengths are noted and celebrated.
- ☐ Patterns and trends are identified and analyzed.
- ☐ Solutions are proposed and negotiated.
- ☐ Commitment to action is obtained from team members.

Video 2.4
A team works through the Data Analysis protocol
qrs.ly/3hghobg

Module 2: Where Are We Now?

QUICK START

	I can start this tomorrow	I can begin this month	I need to discuss this with others	Resources needed
Gather qualitative—not just quantitative—data to analyze collaboratively.				
Gather data that come from a variety of sources, not just test scores and student work.				
Consider a broad array of influences on the results you review that include academic, social, and community factors.				
Maintain openness to the viewpoints of others, including those that are different from yours.				
Review the Data Analysis Protocol, and reflect on which steps or components align with the work your team has already been doing and which aspects are new or unfamiliar to the team.				

Available for download at **https://companion.corwin.com/courses/PLC**

CASE IN POINT: MOVING FROM DEFICIT THINKING TO NEXT-STEPS INSTRUCTION

The ninth- and tenth-grade math teachers at North Central High School sat at a conference table, looking over the latest assessment data. Kim Chu, the algebra teacher, frowned as she scanned the scores. "It's hard to ignore how many of my students are still struggling with factoring. I feel like we're trying everything, and it's just not clicking for them."

Raul Gomez, who teaches geometry, nodded, his expression grim. "I'm seeing similar issues with proofs. A lot of students seem to be giving up as soon as it gets challenging. I feel like this data just highlights how far we still have to go."

Rina Patel, an algebra teacher, took a deep breath. "I get it. These results can be disheartening. But what if we tried to look for the strengths in the data first? Maybe there's something we can build on," she suggested.

After a pause, Raul replied, "You're right, Rina. I just don't know where to start. When I look at these numbers, all I see are gaps and struggles."

Kim chimed back in, saying, "Maybe we need to focus on the areas where students showed even a little progress. It might help us understand what's working, even in small ways."

Rina nodded. "Exactly. Let's try reframing our questions. What are students understanding well, even if it's not across the board? And what might those successes tell us about how we can approach the more challenging areas?"

What's Your Advice?

- Rina's comment was an important pivot for the team, and an example of a member being an activator of the thinking of the group. How would you help this team shift from a deficits-based to a strengths-based approach as they analyze their data?

- What questions could they ask themselves to gain a deeper understanding of their students' progress and potential?

- The team is primarily looking at quantitative data right now. What recommendations would you offer to them to gather qualitative data?

Video 2.5
An activator reflects on the case in point
qrs.ly/ldghobk

CROSSCUTTING VALUES CHECK

How are the educational experiences of all learners informing curriculum, instruction, and assessment at your school? Consider these reflective questions to spark discussion with colleagues.

Equity and Fairness

- In what ways are data gathering and analysis influenced by deficits-based thinking? By strengths-based thinking?
- Do we use a process to analyze the data of all students, including students with disabilities, multilingual learners, and advanced learners?
- Are the data we are analyzing correlated to structural or institutional systems, such as placement, curriculum, interventions, PBIS, MTSS, or other informal or formal programs?
- Are barriers and removal of barriers discussed?

High Expectations

- Are we gathering qualitative and quantitative data on grade-level expectations?
- How do students describe our expectations? What are their expectations for themselves?
- How do families describe our expectations for their students?

Individual and Collective Efficacy

- In what ways do we ensure that we take time to notice and reflect on current student data? What measures do we take to prevent being reactive to data?
- How prevalent is a shared responsibility for student learning (not just the students on my roster) in our professional learning community?
- How can we create an environment of mutual support and accountability to boost both individual and team efficacy?

Activators

- What are some ways we can ensure that our initial assessments capture a range of student strengths and entry points?
- Does this assessment reveal not only students' current understanding but also their misconceptions or gaps in foundational knowledge?
- How can we ensure that our assessment practices reflect our collective goals and values?

SELF-ASSESSMENT

After a direction of travel toward teaching goals has been established through discussions based on question 1: ("Where Are We Going?"), PLC+ teams engage in initial assessments of student learning. After all, there is no point in teaching something that students already know. It is important to note that this new question is prone to biases about student learning and particular groups of students. Thus, we must become aware of those biases and recognize them when they infiltrate any part of the PLC+ initiative.

Rapid Assessment:

We collect and analyze evidence to understand our students, identify equity gaps, challenge bias, and define common challenges that unite our efforts and support collective efficacy.

1	2	3	4	5
Not Begun or Not Initiated	Very Limited Evidence of Capacity	Some Evidence of Capacity	Evidence of Capacity and Limited Evidence of Effective Implementation	Evidence of Capacity and Demonstrated Effective Implementation

Queries for Conducting a Detailed Assessment:

	Where Are We Now?	Not Begun or Not Initiated	Very Limited Evidence of Capacity	Some Evidence of Capacity	Evidence of Capacity and Limited Evidence of Effective Implementation	Evidence of Capacity and Demonstrated Effective Implementation
2.1	We regularly collect data and analyze student work of multiple types.	1	2	3	4	5
2.2	We regularly and effectively discuss the results of our student work analysis as a team.	1	2	3	4	5
2.3	Our data collection and analysis of student work and performance includes identification of equity gaps.	1	2	3	4	5
2.4	Our data collection and analysis of student work, as well as collegial discussion, includes addressing bias.	1	2	3	4	5
2.5	We regularly identify common challenges that can be addressed as a team.	1	2	3	4	5

Available for download at https://companion.corwin.com/courses/PLC

NOTICE AND REFLECT

 ESSENTIAL QUESTION

How does knowing students' current performance support their learning journey?

THINK ABOUT

- Are we ensuring that we know our students' current performance and they know it as well?
- Do we use a rich array of assessment data, or do we stick with a limited number of formats?
- Do we have a process for analyzing data, or do we only look quickly at test scores?

START – STOP – KEEP

Based on what you learned in this module, answer the questions below.

Start: What practice(s) would you like to start doing?

Stop: What practice(s) would you like to stop doing?

Keep: What practice(s) would you like to keep doing?

NOTES

How do we move learning forward?

3 HOW DO WE MOVE LEARNING FORWARD?

The art and science of teaching represent the convergence of two kinds of knowledge. As we discussed in the previous modules, the first influence involves knowing where students are going and where they are now. The second influence is knowledge of evidence-based teaching practices. These include the advanced skills we need to get students to the learning destination. Importantly, neither influence ultimately matters in the absence of the other. To use the metaphor of home construction, a blueprint for a house without the skills to build it means the house is never erected. On the other hand, building skills are wasted if there is no plan for what the final product should look like.

Effective PLC+ teams devote time to quality instruction, not just curriculum and assessment. Much like a tripod with three equal legs, instruction, curriculum, and assessment work in concert with one another to create a stable structure. A professional learning community model that does not dedicate time to understanding evidence-based instruction destabilizes the learning tripod. If we are to truly accelerate student learning, then we must have a plan and the skills to execute the plan.

This phase of the investigation cycle embodies Liberatory Design's *imagine* mode by encouraging teams to "lead innovative approaches and solutions to equity challenges."[56]

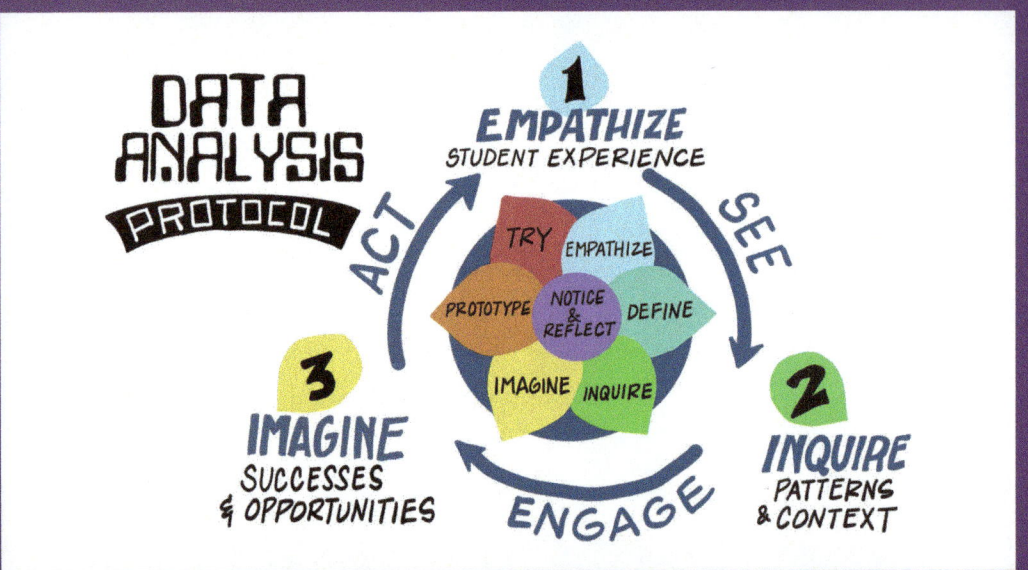

Adapted from "Liberatory Design for Equity" by the National Equity Project. Derived from Anaissie, T., Cary, V., Clifford, D., Malarkey, T. & Wise, S. (2021). Liberatory Design. www.liberatorydesign.com.

 **Essential Question**

HOW DO WE APPLY EVIDENCE-BASED INSTRUCTION TO ACCELERATE LEARNING?

Video 3.1
An elementary team discusses question 3
qrs.ly/odghobn

Video 3.2
A secondary team discusses question 3
qrs.ly/oqghobp

TWO TRUTHS AND A LIE

Two of these statements are true; one is false. Can you spot the lie?

1. Instructional strategies should be aligned with phases of learning: surface, deep, or transfer.

2. How students are grouped is linked to the teacher's expectations for student learning.

3. Acceleration is just another way of describing remediation.

The first statement is true. The phases of learning—surface, deep, and transfer—each play a distinct role in students' mastery of knowledge and skills and are associated with different types of instructional strategies.[57] In the *surface phase*, students are introduced to foundational concepts and basic skills, often through direct instruction, which allows them to acquire essential facts and vocabulary. This initial phase is critical as it establishes the groundwork needed for more complex understanding. As students move into the *deep phase*, they begin to connect ideas, recognize patterns, and apply critical thinking to build a more comprehensive understanding of the content. This phase often involves analyzing relationships between concepts, which promotes a deeper level of cognition. Finally, in the *transfer phase*, students are encouraged to apply their knowledge and skills in new and varied contexts, demonstrating their ability to use what they've learned in real-world situations or across different subjects. This phase is crucial for developing adaptive expertise, as students learn to generalize and adapt their learning to solve novel problems.

The second statement is also true. Grouping decisions are associated with achievement. One study of 3,748 kindergarten multilingual students in mathematics found that in classrooms using homogenous grouping (language learners grouped together) or only whole-class instruction resulted in lower levels of student learning. Mixed and flexible grouping of students resulted in higher student achievement.[58]

The last statement is the lie. Acceleration and remediation are distinct approaches to supporting student learning gaps, but they differ in focus and impact. Remediation often involves reteaching previous skills or knowledge in isolation, aiming to bring students up to grade level by addressing past deficiencies. In contrast, acceleration focuses on preparing students for upcoming content by providing targeted, just-in-time support that connects prerequisite skills directly to current learning goals. Unlike remediation, which can slow students down by revisiting old material, acceleration encourages students to move forward with their peers, building on prior knowledge to access new, grade-level content more successfully.[59] While remediation may be warranted in select cases, it should never be the default intervention approach for any student currently working below grade level.

THE STORY BEHIND THE QUESTION (HOW DO WE MOVE LEARNING FORWARD?)

This question distinguishes PLC+ investigation cycles from the processes conventionally used in older models. The research on evidence-based instruction is drawn from decades of work in schools. Barak Rosenshine, an educational psychologist, developed his influential *10 Principles of Instruction* based on extensive research in cognitive science and observations of successful teaching practices.[60] These ten principles, which we share below, emphasize practical, evidence-based methods that teams can use to enhance student understanding and retention, and they offer a framework to guide teachers in creating effective, structured lessons to move learning forward.

1. **Begin with a daily review.** Each lesson begins with a brief review of previously covered material, activating background knowledge and preparing students for the learning to come.

2. **Present new material in small steps.** Breaking down information into smaller, manageable chunks prevents cognitive overload and allows students to process new information effectively.

3. **Ask questions.** High-quality questioning throughout the lesson is crucial for student engagement and understanding.

4. **Provide models.** Modeling—such as think-alouds, worked examples, direct instruction, or demonstrations—gives students a clear understanding of what success looks like.

5. **Guide student practice.** After introducing new material, teachers provide structured opportunities for students to practice with guidance.

6. **Check for understanding.** Regularly checking to determine what students understand and what they still need to learn allows the teacher to make adjustments in the learning experience.

7. **Obtain a high success rate.** By aiming for a high success rate, ideally around 80 percent, students develop confidence as their competence grows.

8. **Provide scaffolds for difficult tasks.** Scaffolding, such as providing prompts or breaking down steps, supports students as they work through complex material. Gradually removing these supports helps students build independence.

9. **Require independent practice.** Repetition through independent practice solidifies learning, giving students the chance to apply skills without guidance.

10. **Engage in weekly and monthly review.** Regular reviews of past material help reinforce learning and prevent forgetting.

These principles of instruction support all students' learning. They provide a clear, research-backed structure for effective teaching, emphasizing teacher clarity, practice, and continuous assessment, and they serve as a practical guide for enhancing student learning and support cognitive growth. In a PLC+ model, discussion of evidence-based instruction holds a crucial space in every investigation cycle.

Video 3.3
Nancy discusses the story behind question 3
qrs.ly/k9ghobr

NOTES

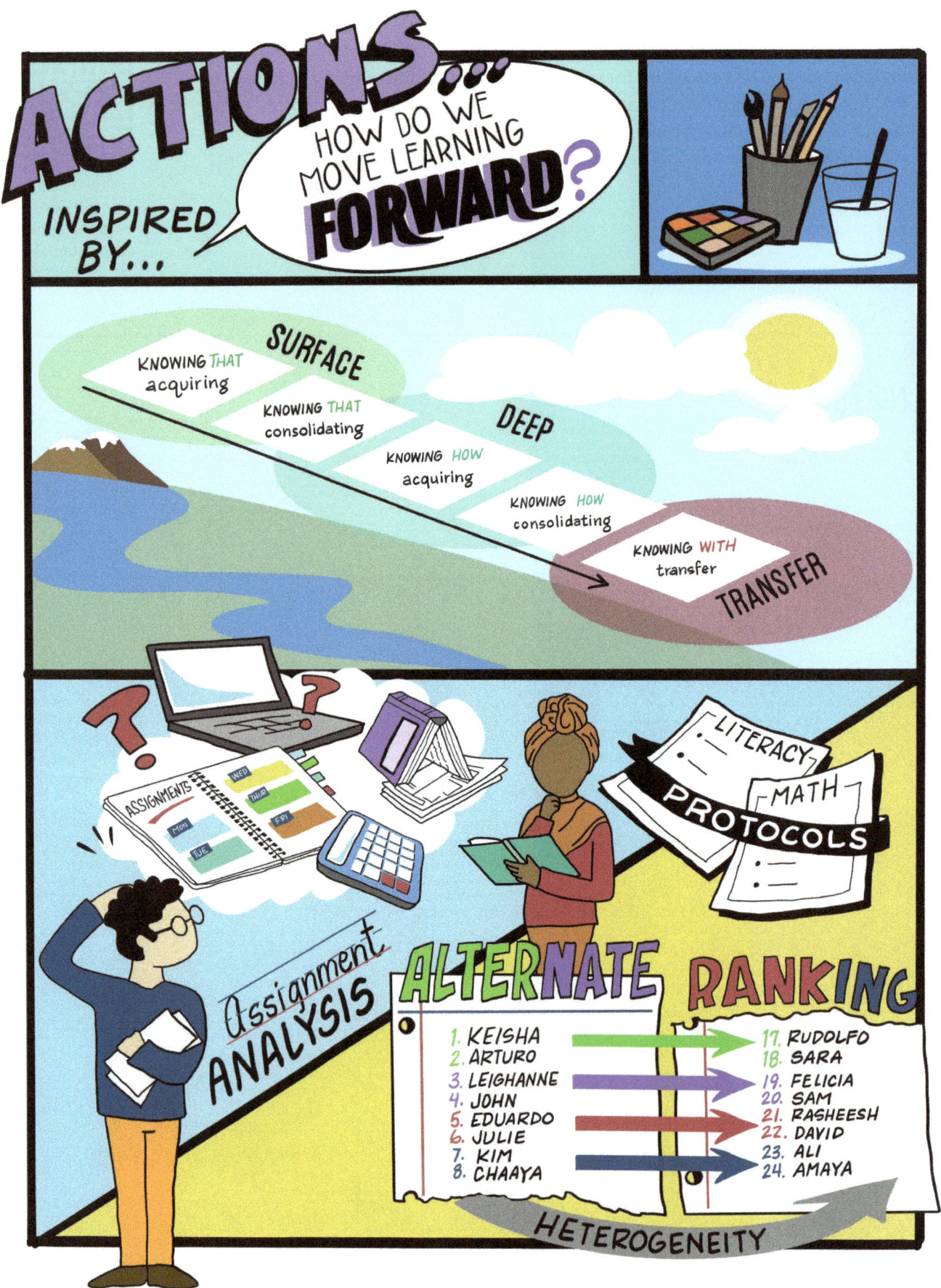

EVIDENCE-BASED INSTRUCTIONAL STRATEGIES

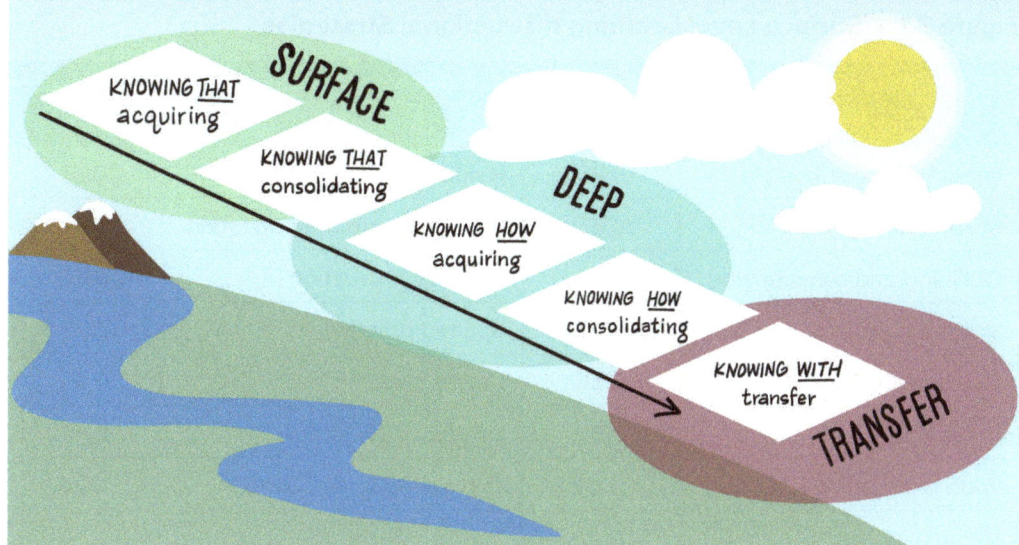

The Visible Learning database is a comprehensive synthesis of over 2,100 studies (meta-analyses) in education, examining factors that impact student achievement.[61] These meta-analyses are grouped into what we have called "mega meta-analyses" that compile findings from millions of students worldwide to identify and quantify the effects of various teaching strategies, practices, and influences on learning. John Hattie's research introduced the concept of effect size as a way to compare the efficacy of various educational interventions, with a threshold of 0.40 (known as the "hinge point") indicating a high potential to accelerate learning and thereby impact student progress. The Visible Learning database provides educators with an evidence-based framework to understand what works best in classrooms, helping them make informed decisions to enhance student outcomes and move learning forward.

WHAT WORKS WHEN?

Now let's pair these influences on learning with what we know about surface, deep, and transfer phases of learning, as discussed at the start of this module, and the importance of correctly aligning instructional strategies to these three phases. As the illustration above shows, surface- and deep-learning phases are divided further into acquiring and consolidating learning stages.

Students benefit from instruction aligned with their current learning phase, with teachers aiming not only for improved knowledge but also for enhanced attitudes and engagement in learning.[62] In a nutshell, different strategies work best at various stages of learning. Doubling down on surface-level instructional strategies will not somehow result in deep learning.

Figure 3.1 contains common instructional strategies useful in developing students' surface-level learning. Remember, surface-level learning is important but not sufficient to ensure that students can use the concepts and skills later. However, skipping surface-level learning puts students at risk because they may not see the connections and relationships between ideas and information.

Figure 3.1 • Surface-Level Learning Instructional Strategies

Surface Learning: Acquisition	Effect Size	Surface Learning: Consolidating	Effect Size
Integrating prior knowledge	0.96	Help-seeking	0.73
Mnemonics	0.65	Rehearsal and memorization	0.71
Outlining and summarizing	0.62	Strategy instruction	0.60
Vocabulary instruction	0.62	Spaced practice	0.59
Direct instruction	0.56	Practice testing	0.49
Rereading	0.50	Interleaved practice	0.46
Wide reading	0.50	Test-taking strategies	0.24
Underlining and highlighting	0.42		
Working memory training	0.37		
Notetaking	0.33		

As you review the figure, notice how the instructional strategies shift as students consolidate their surface learning. While acquisition requires direct instruction, consolidation leans on practice.

Now get ready for another shift in instruction: strategies that move students from surface learning into deep learning (Figure 3.2).

Figure 3.2 • Deep-Learning Instructional Strategies

Deep Learning: Acquisition	Effect Size	Deep Learning: Consolidating	Effect Size
Self-judgment and reflection	0.81	Organizing and transforming notes	0.85
Elaboration and organization	0.75	Classroom discussion	0.82
Elaborative interrogation	0.59	Reciprocal teaching	0.74
Strategy monitoring	0.54	Concept mapping	0.62
Metacognitive strategies	0.52	Self-verbalization and self-questioning	0.58
		Study skills	0.50
		Collaborative learning	0.45

Did you feel the shift? You may have noticed that in order to deepen learning, students need to do a lot more schema building through making connections, anchoring concepts to other ideas, and—especially—organizing their thinking more formally. In other words, they need to apply critical thinking skills. And to ensure that our students do so, we must change both our instructional practices and the tasks themselves. Figure 3.3 identifies common instructional strategies that require transfer, generalization, or application of learning.

Figure 3.3 • **Transfer Learning Instructional Strategies**

Transfer Learning	Effect Size
Jigsaw (useful at surface- and deep-learning phases as well)	1.20
Formal discussions (Socratic seminars, debates, and such)	0.82
Peer tutoring/peer learning	0.66
Synthesizing information across texts	0.63
Problem-solving teaching	0.61
Extended writing	0.44

When students are able to transfer their learning to new and novel situations, their knowledge becomes portable. At the transfer level, students are drawing on knowledge within and across subjects, often employing skills and concepts learned in one setting but applying it to another. Importantly, transfer doesn't happen only near the end of the unit; it can and should occur periodically throughout.

ASK A BOT

Chatbots can draft lesson plans, but they perform better when they are told the parameters of the lesson. For example, you can tell your bot to include the Rosenshine components listed near the start of this module (you may need to list them). Or you can tell your bot to plan a lesson based on the 5E model of instruction (Engage, Explore, Explain, Elaborate, and Evaluate),[63] Madeline Hunter's lesson design,[64] or the gradual release of responsibility framework.[65] For example, you could use the following prompt:

> Design lessons plans for five days on the following learning intentions **[INSERT LEARNING INTENTIONS]**. Use the gradual release of responsibility framework from Doug Fisher and Nancy Frey, and include focused instruction, guided instruction, collaborative learning, and independent learning in any order that makes sense but include all four components every day. Also include assessment opportunities for each of the lessons to check for understanding.

QUICK START

	I can start this tomorrow	I can begin this month	I need to discuss this with others	Resources needed
Analyze the instructional strategies at each phase of learning to determine your current level of knowledge.				
Identify the instructional strategies you are less familiar with and learn more about them.				
Consult curriculum materials to see where instructional strategies foster surface learning, deep learning, and transfer of learning.				
Discuss which of the strategies are most culturally relevant and culturally sustaining.				
Reflect on your current practice for grouping students. How do you decide who works with whom, and what does that grouping structure indicate about teachers' beliefs and expectations?				
Review Rosenshine's principles of instruction. As you collaborate with your PLC team to plan instruction, identify which of these principles are most frequently discussed and which ones may need more focus or attention in your planning process.				

online resources — Available for download at **https://companion.corwin.com/courses/PLC**

ASSIGNMENT ANALYSIS

The Education Trust's assignment analysis tools are designed to help educators evaluate the quality and rigor of classroom literacy and mathematics assignments.[66,67] The protocols developed from their analysis tools assist PLC+ teams in examining whether assignments they are designing align with standards and engage students in meaningful, grade-appropriate work. By focusing on key elements such as cognitive challenge, alignment to standards, and relevance to students' lives, the tool enables educators to assess if assignments are not only helping students build essential skills but also providing equal opportunities for academic growth. In this way, assignment analysis encourages reflection on instructional practices to ensure all students are challenged and prepared for academic success. Specifically, to move learning forward, PLC+ teams can use the protocols either to analyze and update previous assignments so they can be used again in more effective ways or to craft new assignments for an upcoming unit of instruction.

It can be useful for teams to consider how the analysis will take place. In can be beneficial to perform the analysis by using anonymous assignments that are not tied to a particular teacher. Otherwise, it can be awkward and counterproductive to say something like, "Let's all review our colleague Megan's assignment and tell her what we think of it." Instead, start out with reviewing commercially prepared tasks in curriculum materials, and be sure to review several assignments that are representative of the unit as a whole, because a single assignment may not meet all of the criteria. This approach can also provide the team with further insight regarding high-quality instructional materials. As you become comfortable with the protocol, use it proactively to develop future tasks that pair high expectations with high support.

LITERACY ASSIGNMENT ANALYSIS TOOL PROTOCOL

Analyzing the literacy tasks that students are assigned helps teams decide if they are requiring students to practice grade-level expectations using complex texts. Sometimes, small adjustments to the tasks and assignments used in class can increase the rigor of the work and allow students to practice and learn before major assessments.

Purpose: Analyzing tasks for their cognitive complexity and rigor allows teams to decide if they are teaching and assessing standards and to identify opportunities to address unfinished learning.

STEP 1: Determine the key features of the assignment

Text type (literary, informational, visual, multiple texts)	
Text length (excerpt, chapter, etc.)	
Text complexity (quantitative and qualitative values that suggest the grade range of the selected text)	
Writing output (no writing required, note-taking, one or two sentences, multiple short responses, one paragraph, multiple paragraphs)	
Length of assignment (fifteen minutes or less, one to two class periods, multiple weeks, linked to an ongoing project [quarter/semester/year])	
Student thinking *Webb's Depth of Knowledge* [ ] Recall and reproduction [ ] Basic application of skills/concepts [ ] Strategic thinking [ ] Extended thinking	

STEP 2: Assignment analysis

> 1. **Alignment With Standards**
>
> *A standards-aligned assignment has essential features. First and most importantly, it must be grade-level appropriate. The assignment must embrace instructional shifts, including regular practice with complex texts; academic language; read, write, and speak using evidence; and build knowledge through content information. The assignment is clearly articulated so that students can fully understand what is expected of them.*

Assignment Analysis for Alignment With Standards:

2. **Centrality of Text**

The centrality of the text allows students to grapple with key ideas, author's craft and intent, and larger meanings. Students have the opportunity to (1) display increasing expertise in interpreting and responding to text and (2) draw evidence from text to justify their responses and thinking. Specifically, an assignment fully reflects this centrality of text when students are required to cite evidence (e.g., paraphrasing, direct citation) to support a position or claim.

Assignment Analysis for Centrality of Text:

3. **Cognitive Challenge**

The cognitive work that is required to retell a story, identify facts from a text, analyze a character using textual evidence, or apply knowledge gained from multiple texts to form new ideas ranges from simple to complex. Generally, the cognitive challenge increases through text-dependent questions and assignments that require student documentation of their deep analysis or the construction of new knowledge. Use Webb's Depth of Knowledge levels (outlined in Step 1) in your analysis. The expectation of an extended written response (multiple paragraphs), which is governed by the acceptable practices of the discipline, most strongly supports such thinking.

Assignment Analysis for Cognitive Challenge:

4. **Motivation and Engagement**

For learners to thrive and achieve at high levels, educators must embrace both the content of the curriculum and the design of instruction. Each of these elements impacts student attention, interest, motivation, and cognitive effort and must be considered in the design of assignments. Specifically, we prioritize choice and relevancy. Students must be given some level of autonomy and independence in their tasks—with rigor maintained across all options. And the tasks must be relevant as they focus on poignant topics, use real-world materials and experiences, and give students the opportunity to make connections with their goals, interests, and values.

(Continued)

(Continued)

Assignment Analysis for Motivation and Engagement:

STEP 3: Team Discussion

RECOMMENDATIONS FOR STRENGTHENING THE ASSIGNMENT	
Use this space to focus on improving aspects of the assignment that need more attention.	
1. Alignment With Standards	
2. Centrality of Text	
3. Cognitive Challenge	
4. Motivation and Engagement	

Adapted from *Checking in: Do classroom assignments reflect today's higher standards?* Sonja Brookins Santelises, Education Trust. (2015).

Video 3.4
A team works through the ELA assignment analysis protocol
qrs.ly/78ghobt

NOTES

MATH ASSIGNMENT ANALYSIS TOOL PROTOCOL

Analyzing the mathematics assignments that students are assigned helps teams decide if they are requiring students to practice grade-level expectations using rich tasks. Sometimes, small adjustments to the tasks and assignments used in class can increase the rigor of the work and allow students to practice and learn before major assessments.

Purpose: Analyzing tasks for their cognitive complexity and rigor allows teams to decide if they are teaching and assessing standards and to identify opportunities to address unfinished learning.

STEP 1: Determine the key features of the assignment

What grade level or course does this assignment come from?	
Length of assignment [ ] A short/brief task that is completed in fifteen minutes or less (e.g., do now, warm-up, exit ticket, journal reflection) [ ] A task that is completed within one to two class periods (e.g., performance task, extended discussion) [ ] A task that is a long-term, ongoing assignment completed over the duration of multiple weeks (e.g., project, research analysis)	

STEP 2: Assignment analysis

ALIGNMENT	
Does the assignment focus on the depth of grade-level cluster(s), grade-level content standard(s), or part(s) thereof?	
What is the primary content standard addressed in this assignment?	
Does this assignment build on or connect to additional content standards (within the same grade, from a previous grade or course, or a future grade or course)?	

(Continued)

(Continued)

Does this assignment provide opportunities to incorporate the Standards for Mathematical Practice? Check all that apply: [ ] Make sense of problems and persevere in solving them [ ] Reason abstractly and quantitatively [ ] Construct viable arguments and critique the reasoning of others [ ] Model with mathematics [ ] Use appropriate tools strategically [ ] Attend to precision [ ] Look for and make use of structure [ ] Look for and express regularity in repeated reasoning [ ] Accurately use mathematics and academic vocabulary	
Does the assignment clearly articulate the task?	

COGNITIVE CHALLENGE	
What is the level of cognitive demand required by the assignment? [ ] *Recall and Reproduction*: Recall a fact, term, principle, concept; perform a routine procedure or a simple algorithm; or apply a formula [ ] *Basic Application of Skills/Concepts*: Use information, apply conceptual knowledge, select appropriate procedures for a task, complete two or more steps with decision points along the way, complete routine problems, organize/display data, or interpret/use sample data [ ] *Strategic Thinking*: Requires reasoning or developing a plan or sequence of steps to approach the problem; requires some decision-making and justification; it's abstract, complex, or nonroutine; and there is often more than one possible answer [ ] *Extended Thinking*: An investigation or application to the real world; requires time to research, problem solve, and process multiple conditions of the problem or task; and requires nonroutine manipulations across disciplines/content areas/multiple sources	

ASPECTS OF RIGOR	
Which aspect(s) of rigor does the assignment address? Check all that apply: [ ] *Conceptual Understanding*: The assignment provides an opportunity for conceptual understanding of key concepts; allows for accessing the concept from a number of perspectives in order to see math as more than a set of mnemonics or discrete procedures [ ] *Procedural Skills and Fluency*: The assignment provides an opportunity for practice of core functions, solving equations with speed and accuracy in calculation [ ] *Application*: The assignment provides an opportunity to use math flexibly for applications in problem-solving contexts	

ASPECTS OF RIGOR	
Does this assignment provide multiple representations of mathematical concepts and/or equations?	
Does this assignment develop students' conceptual, representational, and/or abstract understanding?	

COMMUNICATING MATHEMATICAL UNDERSTANDING	
Does the assignment require students to communicate their understanding using the language of mathematics?	
What is the writing output of the assignment? [ ] No writing or communication [ ] Writing short phrases, up to two sentences [ ] Writing one or more paragraphs	
How is discussion incorporated into this assignment? [ ] No evidence of discussion in this assignment [ ] The assignment includes cues/moments for informal and/or brief discussion [ ] The assignment includes cues/significant time for formal and/or extended discussion	

(Continued)

(Continued)

What is the central purpose of the discussion within the assignment? [ ] No evidence of discussion in the assignment [ ] The central purpose is to clarify the tasks or manage the logistics within the assignment (e.g., students discuss the plan for the assignment, students talk with a partner if they need help/clarification) [ ] The central purpose aligns with a Speaking and Listening Standard and is anchored by course content (e.g., students contribute accurate and relevant information, students present knowledge and ideas using evidence and a clear line of reasoning, students consider and evaluate the ideas of others)	
MOTIVATION AND ENGAGEMENT	
Do students have choice in the assignment in one of the following areas: content, product, process, or tools? Is rigor maintained across all options?	
Is the task relevant; does it focus on a poignant topic, use real-world materials, and/or give students the freedom to make connections to their experiences, goals, interests, and values?	
SCAFFOLDING	
What is the amount of teacher supports and/or scaffolds in this assignment? a) No scaffolding in this assignment b) Minimal/moderate scaffolding in this assignment (e.g., scaffolding appears in one section of the assignment, scaffolding appears in less than half of the assignment) c) Heavy scaffolding in this assignment (e.g., scaffolding is ongoing in the assignment, scaffolding is present in more than half of the assignment)	
What is the type of scaffolding in this assignment? Check all that apply: [ ] No scaffolding in this assignment [ ] This assignment itself is a scaffold (e.g., students complete a graphic organizer, students take notes) [ ] This assignment is broken down into small bits/chunks (e.g., students work on very small tasks, such as individual, discrete steps to solve a math problem) [ ] The heavy cognitive work has already been given to students in this assignment (e.g., the process, strategy, or math tools have been laid out for students)	

STEP 3: TEAM DISCUSSION

RECOMMENDATIONS FOR STRENGTHENING THE ASSIGNMENT	
Use this space to focus on improving aspects of the assignment that need more attention.	
1. Alignment With Standards	
2. Cognitive Challenge	
3. Aspects of Rigor	
4. Communicating Mathematical Understanding	
5. Motivation and Engagement	
6. Scaffolding	

Adapted from *Checking in: Are math assignments measuring up?* Keith Dysarz, Education Trust. (2018).

Video 3.5
A team works through the mathematics
assignment analysis protocol
qrs.ly/2ughobu

ASK A BOT

Once you become familiar with the protocols, you can load the assignment analysis tool into your favorite chatbot and set this as your success criteria. Then load an existing assignment your team would like to redesign and ask for ideas for improvement. A sample prompt might look something like this:

> We are tenth-grade Modern World History teachers developing a unit called Connecting Hemispheres. I have attached our table of specifications for the unit and the standards to be addressed. We are designing a series of in-class assignments for our students to use during this three-week unit. Our success criteria for robust assignments are informed by the Education Trust literacy

(Continued)

(Continued)

assignment tool, which is also attached. Suggest three text-based in-class assignments that we can use. Be sure to include discussion as a part of the assignments.

The value is in the dialogic nature of working with the bot. When we tried this exercise ourselves, after several rounds of dialogue with the bot, we got three assignments that might be of value to help our students move forward. Here's one:

Assignment 2: The Black Death as a Catalyst for Change

Learning Intention: Explore the social, political, and economic effects of the Black Death.

1. **Preparation (10 minutes)**
   - Introduce the historical context with a brief teacher-led discussion: "How might a massive pandemic like the Black Death disrupt the established order in medieval Europe?"
   - Provide students with *The Ordinance of Labourers (1349)* and a secondary source excerpt.

2. **Task (25 minutes)**
   - Students work in groups to complete a cause-and-effect chart categorizing the Black Death's short- and long-term impacts (social, political, economic). Groups identify specific textual evidence for each category.

3. **Discussion (20 minutes)**
   - Groups share their charts with the class, presenting one significant effect and supporting evidence. Facilitate a discussion on connections between the effects (e.g., how social changes influenced political shifts).

4. **Output**
   - Students individually write a paragraph explaining how the Black Death acted as a catalyst for change, using group discussions and textual evidence.

We're not Modern World History teachers, and it is quite possible that this assignment could be further improved by content experts. However, the initial assignments offer a toehold for the team to discuss and refine. Expand this discussion by identifying the phase of learning (surface? deep? transfer?) and developing aligned instructional strategies that accelerate the learning.

QUICK START

	I can start this tomorrow	I can begin this month	I need to discuss this with others	Resources needed
Practice using the assignment analysis tool with assignments already in curricular materials.				
Identify several assignments over the course of the unit to gain a fair picture of alignment to standards and depth of knowledge needed.				
Apply the guidelines for robust assignments to develop new tasks.				
Seek feedback from focal students regarding assignments developed for this investigation cycle. Try using the assignment analysis protocol with a new or upcoming assignment.				
Review the components of the assignment analysis tool to identify trends in missing or underdeveloped elements. Are there specific areas that are consistently strong or consistently lacking (e.g., student choice is often missing, but extended writing is frequently included)?				

online resources Available for download at **https://companion.corwin.com/courses/PLC**

ALTERNATE RANKING TO GROUP STUDENTS FOR SUCCESS

Adapted from Frey, N., Fisher, D., & Hattie, J. (2018)

Flexible, heterogeneous grouping of students is a powerful instructional strategy that promotes equity and fosters academic growth for all learners. Christina Rubie-Davies's research on high-expectations teaching highlights the importance of inclusive practices that avoid segregating students by perceived ability, which can reinforce inequities and limit potential.[68] Heterogeneous grouping allows students currently performing at different academic levels to work together, which creates opportunities for peer learning and mutual support. Students benefit from diverse perspectives and experiences, which enrich discussions and problem-solving activities. By using flexible groups that change based on the task, teachers can ensure that all students are exposed to rigorous content and are held to high expectations, essential principles of Rubie-Davies's framework.

As we have noted, teacher beliefs about students' potential significantly influence learning outcomes. The grouping practices of high-expectation teachers (HETs) versus low-expectation teachers (LETs) differ, and they reflect teachers' views about student differences. HETs focus on motivation, while LETs focus on ability. HETs grouped students heterogeneously to improve motivation and creativity, while LETs used ability grouping to alter lessons, which created disparate learning opportunities.[69]

Flexible grouping prevents the fixed labels often associated with ability grouping and tracking, which can negatively impact students' self-efficacy and motivation. While some educators may believe they are preserving the self-esteem of low-performing students by placing them in ability groups, the opposite is true. Low-performing students in ability-grouped classrooms demonstrate negative self-beliefs.[70] In mixed-ability settings, students who might struggle in one area can still contribute strengths in others, fostering confidence and a growth mindset. Meanwhile, higher-performing students deepen their understanding by explaining concepts to peers. This dynamic environment encourages teachers to maintain high expectations for all students, ensuring that no one is left behind or unchallenged as we strive to move learning forward.

Educators can broaden students' interactions to give students access to others in their classroom and to promote heterogeneous grouping. For example, you can use an alternate ranking system to arrange table groups such that social and academic skills are promoted across the classroom. You can also group students for collaborative tasks by following these steps:

1. Rank the class by their relevant skill level, from the top-performing student to the lowest-performing student.
2. Cut that list at the midpoint.
3. Forms groups by selecting students from each half of the list.

For instance, one teacher listed the thirty-two students in order of skill based on the most recent formative assessment. She then cut the list in half after student 16, so the second half of the list comprised the names of students 17 through 32. She then placed both halves side by side and paired the first two names from the first half with the top two names from the second half. Therefore students 1, 2, 17, and 18 were grouped together; students 3, 4, 19, and 20 were grouped together; and so on.

In this way, every group maintains heterogeneity, but the skills of the members within the group are not so different from one another that the group cannot produce. Maintaining a balance of current performance levels within each group is important so that students who are currently performing well do not take over the task and limit the participation (and learning) of the other students.

NOTES

QUICK START

	I can start this tomorrow	I can begin this month	I need to discuss this with others	Resources needed
Evaluate your current grouping system. When was the last time you changed groupings?				
Learn more about the research on mixed-ability grouping benefits.				
Determine a way to rank students (e.g., academic score, skill expertise, prosocial skills), and develop new groups.				
Identify how you will determine the effects of your new grouping approach. For instance, how can your focal students assist you in making this determination?				
Consider how a grouping strategy could support or hinder the student learning.				

online resources — Available for download at **https://companion.corwin.com/courses/PLC**

CASE IN POINT: SURFACE VERSUS DEEP LEARNING

A PLC+ team at Lincoln Middle School met to discuss how to move learning forward. Holly Dalhouse, the sixth-grade English teacher, began the discussion. "Alright, team, our common challenge is on improving argumentation writing. What's been working for you all? My students do okay with claims, but their evidence is weak."

Jonathan Spencer, a seventh-grade social studies teacher, said, "I've been using fill-in-the-blank templates. You know, 'My claim is ___. My evidence is ___. My reasoning is ___.' It helps them get started."

"I do something similar with sentence starters," said Brandi Winston, an eighth-grade science teacher. "They're great for scaffolding. But honestly, my students still just repeat facts from the text. I think we need to drill them on identifying key details better."

The special educator, Jesse Reyes, asked, "What about a lot of practice tests? If they keep answering text-dependent questions, they'll get better at pulling evidence, right? Maybe even a few mnemonics to help them remember claim-evidence-reasoning."

"Exactly," said Ms. Dalhouse. "I've also been giving them model paragraphs to copy for structure. If they mimic good arguments enough, I think it will click eventually."

"But are we overcomplicating it?" asked Mr. Spencer. "I feel like we just need to stick to basics—definitions of claims, evidence, and reasoning. If they memorize those, it's a good foundation."

"True," commented Mr. Reyes, "but are we pushing them enough? Sometimes I wonder if we're just preparing them to repeat the same ideas without really analyzing."

The group hesitated, glancing at each other. They knew they were focused on surface-level strategies—mnemonics, sentence starters, and practice testing—but no one suggested a deeper approach. The conversation stalled, leaving the challenge unresolved.

What's Your Advice?

- Mr. Reyes's last comment was hovering on the cusp of being an activator. How might he turn the team's attention back to a discussion of surface versus deep phases of learning?

- The team seems to be stuck on more practice, which is useful for consolidating what students already know. But what's missing are student reflection and discussion, which are associated with deep learning. What suggestions might you have for ways they could make these happen in their classrooms?

- Also missing are any practices to foster transfer. Choose an instructional approach associated with transfer of learning, and apply it to this scenario.

Video 3.6
An activator reflects on the case in point
qrs.ly/uwghobw

CROSSCUTTING VALUES CHECK

What is the status of consistency in instruction designed to move learning forward at your school? Consider these reflective questions to spark discussion with colleagues.

Equity and Fairness

- What is our evidence that our focal students are benefiting from instructional strategies designed to deepen learning?
- Do we have regular conversations about surface, deep, and transfer levels of learning?
- Do we routinely analyze assignments?

High Expectations

- What evidence of high-expectations teaching is manifested in our instruction? In our grouping practices?
- In what ways are high expectations paired with high support for students?
- Do we focus on acceleration, or do we only discuss remediation?

Individual and Collective Efficacy

- To what extent do teachers who are new to the profession or new to the school benefit from the work of our PLC+ teams?
- How can we ensure that evidence-based instruction is used to support our collective goals?
- What future professional learning should occur as a result of our investigation cycle? What school/district support and resources exist to help us engage in professional learning?

Activators

- Which moments in our PLC+ team meetings have been successful? Where do we want to strengthen our team?
- How do we get ourselves back on track and refocused on our common challenge when we stray away from the purpose?
- How am I investing in my own learning?

SELF-ASSESSMENT

Now that we have dedicated time and effort to defining where we are going (Module 1) as well as to identifying where we are now (Module 2), we focus on the direction of travel. In other words, how will we, and our students, make progress toward our destination? When faced with many ways to reach a given destination, how does the PLC+ team effectively plan? To successfully attend to this question, teams must leverage their answers to the first two questions into intentional decisions about what will work best to move learning forward. It might also be limited to simply changing the current approaches to teaching. Or it could require addressing both elements.

Rapid Assessment:

We match evidence-based instructional approaches to defined learning needs and assess and increase our own abilities to deliver instruction.

1	2	3	4	5
Not Begun or Not Initiated	Very Limited Evidence of Capacity	Some Evidence of Capacity	Evidence of Capacity and Limited Evidence of Effective Implementation	Evidence of Capacity and Demonstrated Effective Implementation

Queries for Conducting a Detailed Assessment:

	How Do We Move Learning Forward?	Not Begun or Not Initiated	Very Limited Evidence of Capacity	Some Evidence of Capacity	Evidence of Capacity and Limited Evidence of Effective Implementation	Evidence of Capacity and Demonstrated Effective Implementation
3.1	We regularly identify and match evidence-based instructional approaches to identified needs and priorities.	1	2	3	4	5
3.2	We identify and implement strategies aligned with phases of learning.	1	2	3	4	5
3.3	We systematically assess the impact of our instructional choices on students' learning.	1	2	3	4	5
3.4	We regularly analyze assignments against rigor criteria.	1	2	3	4	5
3.5	We regularly assess our own abilities and learning needs, in addition to our students' performance levels.	1	2	3	4	5

 Available for download at **https://companion.corwin.com/courses/PLC**

NOTICE AND REFLECT

ESSENTIAL QUESTION

How do we apply evidence-based instruction to accelerate learning?

THINK ABOUT

- Do we understand and use principles of learning, such as those proposed by Rosenshine?
- Do we understand phases of learning? Do our instructional practices align with this understanding?
- Do we analyze assignments as part of our high-quality instructional materials?
- Do we use flexible, mixed-ability grouping regularly?
- Do we involve focal students in monitoring our instructional impact?

START – STOP – KEEP

Based on what you learned in this module, answer the questions below.

Start: What practice(s) would you like to start doing?

Stop: What practice(s) would you like to stop doing?

Keep: What practice(s) would you like to keep doing?

NOTES

WHAT DID WE LEARN TODAY?

4 WHAT DID WE LEARN TODAY?

A prototype is a preliminary model of a product, system, or concept used to test and validate ideas, functionality, and design. It serves as a tool for gathering feedback, identifying flaws, and refining the final version. As educators, we are continually prototyping new ideas in order to improve students' learning. But the potential value of a prototype is lost if we are not able to notice and reflect. In the language of Liberatory Design, the *prototype* mode allows teams to "build rough versions of what you're working on to test key ideas." In the PLC+ model, prototyping rapidly moves into the *try* mode as we apply the prototype we have developed and gather feedback.

The question we'll focus on throughout this module—"What did we learn today?"—is a reminder that we must seek to learn from one another as we prototype and revise our efforts. It requires, as always, that we notice and reflect on what we are learning. But if we remain largely on our own, then our ability to notice is limited, and our ability to reflect is diminished because we don't have access to the thinking of others. The actions associated with this question seek to interrupt institutional barriers, many of which were learned and perpetuated by claims stating, "That's how we've always done it." The barrier this question seeks to eliminate is the self-imposed one that suppresses our urge to collaborate meaningfully with one another, especially the reluctance to open our practice to our peers. This phase in the investigation cycle is about us.

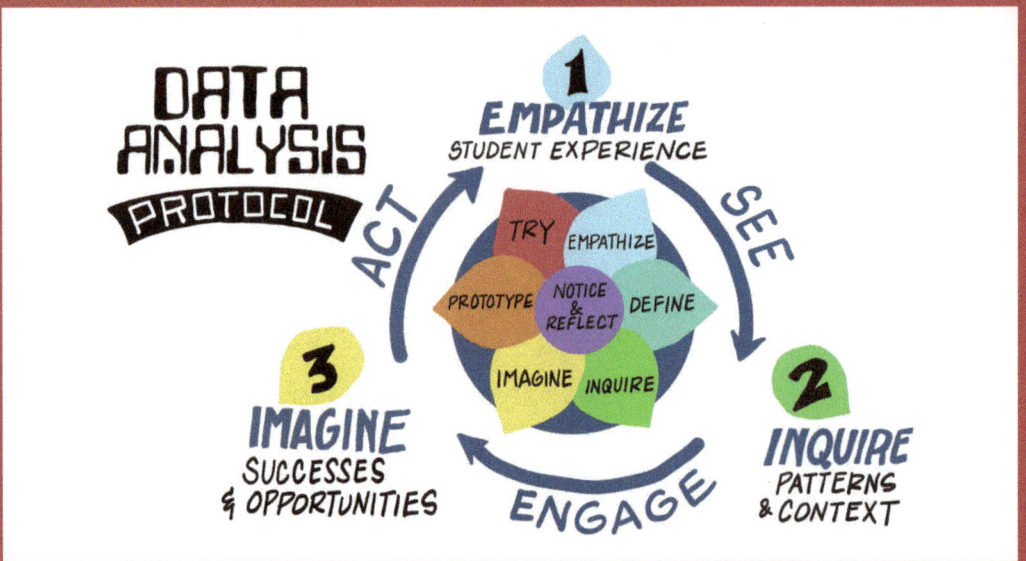

Adapted from "Liberatory Design for Equity" by the National Equity Project. Derived from Anaissie, T., Cary, V., Clifford, D., Malarkey, T. & Wise, S. (2021). Liberatory Design. www.liberatorydesign.com.

Essential Question

HOW DO WE LEARN ABOUT OUR EFFORTS TO IMPACT STUDENT LEARNING AND SHARE THAT INFORMATION WITH OTHERS?

Video 4.1
An elementary team discusses question 4
qrs.ly/lsghobx

Video 4.2
A secondary team discusses question 4
qrs.ly/1bghoc0

TWO TRUTHS AND A LIE

***Two of these statements are true; one is false.
Can you spot the lie?***

1. Teachers with a higher degree of self-reported wellness attribute some of their success to meaningful gatherings with colleagues.

2. Ninth-grade students who attend schools with high collective teacher efficacy are more likely to be on track for graduation at the end of ninth grade.

3. Trust between colleagues is best grown when teachers avoid engaging in critical dialogue with one another.

The first statement is true. A study of high school teachers found that those with higher levels of well-being noted that meaningful gatherings with colleagues contributed to their crisis efficacy—their confidence and ability to adapt to unprecedented challenges.[71] Meaningful connections with our colleagues, especially connections that allow us to accomplish tasks and feel supported, increase the likelihood that we value our work and experience lower levels of stress.

The second statement is also true. In high schools with low measures of teacher self-efficacy or collective teacher efficacy, students are less likely to be on track at the end of ninth grade than those peers in schools with a high degree of teacher self-efficacy and collective teacher efficacy.[72] Importantly, measures of ambitious instruction proved to be a mediating factor in the successful schools that were studied. The researchers noted that the ninth-grade teams that were focused on a freshmen success initiative were able to "help facilitate collective self-efficacy since they provide the opportunity for teachers to learn from each other, problem solve, and center on a common goal."[73]

Of course, the last statement is false—but for a really interesting reason. A researcher named Timothy Ford was intrigued by the results of study of the results on the Programme for International Student Assessment (PISA), a measure of fifteen-year-old students in reading, mathematics, and science administered annually across eighty-one countries. The highest-performing countries correlated to higher relational trust within schools.[74] Ford then studied 115 elementary schools in fifteen states to identify the drivers of increased teacher-to-teacher trust. Using quantitative data, he found three conditions contributed to collegial trust: critical dialogue; a climate of innovation and risk-taking; and collective, rather than individual, responsibility for students' learning.

Regarding the first condition, critical dialogue, Ford stated, "High-risk interactions around curriculum and instruction in which teachers engage in critical dialogue and examination of practice are those which scholars suggest have the greatest likelihood of transforming practice and hold the greatest potential for building trust."[75] Although it may seem counterintuitive, critical dialogue—including expressing professional views; being willing to question another's view; and talking through views, opinions, and values—is key to deepening collegial trust. Avoiding challenging conversations, which is called *hindered communication*, does not build trust; in fact, it may actually diminish trust.[76]

THE STORY BEHIND THE QUESTION (WHAT DID WE LEARN TODAY?)

Teams need to talk about the evidence they collect, even if it makes them uncomfortable. The reason that it's important for the team to ask "What have we learned?" is that PLCs need time to discuss—in productive ways—the evidence they collect from students, and to take action based on what the data tell them. Importantly, we can mobilize our collective efficacy through discussions about evidence of student learning.

Sometimes, however, discussions about student learning are less than effective. In fact, there is evidence that a significant percentage of team time spent in data discussions is ineffective and does not result in improved student learning.[77] When teams fail to use protocols or do not have strong activators, they may inadvertently dismiss the data, discussing instead elements such as student behavior, problems with the format of the test, students' home environments, or suspected disabilities, rather than discussing what the team can do as a learning community to move students' learning forward.

Dialogue is the fuel that powers the professional learning community. Consequently, as we have stated, the avoidance of dialogue can hamper the success of a team. A key to effective dialogue is having shared experiences that provide common ground for discussion, thereby fostering trust and collaboration among colleagues. Shared experiences create opportunities to reflect on similar challenges, exchange strategies, and build a collective understanding of effective practices. By drawing on shared experiences, the team is more likely to engage in meaningful, solution-oriented conversations.

With that in mind, shared experiences should not be limited to meetings. As educators, we are not in this profession so that we can refine our meeting skills. Instead, we seek to refine our teaching skills. That means our shared experiences must be classroom-based. We need to see each other in action. Yet in many cases, there is a reluctance to opening up one's practice and observing in other people's classrooms. Do any of these hesitations resonate with you?

- *Fear of judgment.* Teachers may worry about being criticized or judged, particularly if they feel vulnerable about their teaching methods or classroom management.

- *Perceived incompetence.* Some teachers fear appearing less skilled or knowledgeable in front of peers, which may affect their professional confidence or reputation.

- *Lack of trust.* A lack of trust and an absence of strong collegial relationships within a school can make teachers hesitant to share their practices openly.

- *Cultural norms.* In some school environments, teaching is seen as a private act, making peer observation feel intrusive or out of the norm.

Collegial trust must be actively cultivated, maintained, and repaired. Ford's findings, as discussed in the previous section, revealed that three conditions were undertaken by high-trust schools: a willingness to engage in critical dialogue, actions that contribute to a climate of innovation and risk-taking, and a shared responsibility for the learning of all the students in the school, not just the ones on the roster.[78]

In the traffic light exercise below, teams can use Ford's findings to spark their own reflection. Specifically, we invite you to consider the status of actions that build collegial trust in your own school, because collegial trust creates spaces for collaboration.

Using the traffic light scale—with red being very few, yellow being some, and green indicating most—how many teachers at your school engage in critical dialogue, innovation and risk-taking, and shared responsibility?

Critical Dialogue

1. Teachers openly express professional views at meetings.

2. Teachers are willing to question one another's views.

Video 4.3
Doug discusses the story behind question 4
qrs.ly/nlghoc6

3. Teachers do a good job of talking through views, opinions, and values.

Climate of Innovation and Risk-Taking

4. Teachers are expected to continually learn and seek out new ideas.

5. Teachers are encouraged to experiment in their classrooms.

6. Teachers are encouraged to take risks to improve their teaching.

Collective Responsibility

7. Teachers take responsibility for helping one another do well.

8. Teachers help maintain positive student behavior in the entire school.

9. Teachers take responsibility for improving the quality of teaching in the school.

COLLECTING EVIDENCE FROM STUDENTS IN CYCLES

We use assessments formatively when they serve to inform our decisions. Although some teachers argue that assessments take time away from instruction, the truth is that practicing instruction in the absence of assessment is like teaching with our eyes covered. By analyzing the evidence generated through the assessment, we can see what learning is sticking and what is not so we can make informed decisions about next steps. Our definition of assessment used to inform students' learning is this:

> An assessment functions formatively to the extent that evidence about student achievement is elicited; interpreted; and used by teachers, students, or their peers to make decisions about the next steps in instruction that are likely to be better, or better founded, than the decisions they would have taken in the absence of that elicited evidence.[79]

There are several key phrases within the definition that are worth noting:

- *Evidence is elicited, interpreted, and used.* This evidence needs to be collected, but interpretation and application are key. Otherwise, the assessment is of no value.

- *Teachers, students, and peers use it.* In true collaborative design, access is shared and discussed with stakeholders.

- *Evidence is used to make decisions.* The purpose of gathering evidence is to use it to strengthen decisions.

Just as important, but often overlooked, is the reverse: We must engage in *decision-driven data collection*.[80] With every decision the PLC+ team makes, there should be a subsequent decision about what data will be used to monitor its effects. The decisions teams make about data collection should not be haphazard. Instead, the assessment plan should include everything from checks for understanding during a lesson to benchmarks or interim assessments used to monitor progress. Effective teams map the assessments they will use to monitor decisions.

We can view assessment cycles in terms of their duration and purpose, with formative assessment practices categorized as long, medium, or short cycles.

- *Long-cycle formative assessments* occur over periods of six to ten weeks or longer, helping teams to monitor progress toward the attainment of the goals developed through the common challenge and to adjust the instruction to ensure it is in alignment with those goals.

- *Medium-cycle formative assessments* take place within instructional units, engaging students as active participants in the process by clarifying assessment criteria and promoting self-assesssement.

- *Short-cycle formative assessments* happen minute to minute or day to day during lessons, providing immediate feedback to guide our teaching and to help us support student learning in real time (see Figure 4.1).

Figure 4.1 • Three Formative Assessment Cycles

Type	Purpose	Time Span	Examples
Long-Cycle Formative Assessments	Gauge student progress toward mastery of standards Curriculum alignment	6 to 10 weeks or longer	Common formative assessments within or across the building Interim and benchmark assessments
Medium-Cycle Formative Assessments	Gauge student progress toward mastery of unit goals May be used within or between units to make decisions about reteaching or extension and enrichment	2 to 6 weeks	Practice tests, short constructed responses linked to unit goals or success criteria
Short-Cycle Formative Assessments	Gauge student understanding during instruction to inform near-term instructional decisions	Within and between lessons	Checks for understanding (e.g., exit tickets, universal response opportunities, questioning)

Source: Wiliam, D., Fisher, D., & Frey, N. (2024).

ASK A BOT

Chatbots can create assessments quickly, but the risk is that the questions or tasks are literal and limited to surface-level learning. To eliminate that concern, you can tell the bot what type of assessment you are looking for and require that it include a range of question types or task types. For example, you might use the following prompt:

> Create an assessment of students' understanding of the following standard(s) **[INSERT STANDARDS]**. Make sure to include a range of complexity that includes literal and inferential questions and tasks. I need at least _____ items, and there should be a gradual increase in the difficulty of the items. Develop an answer key for each [or rubric if you provide indicators of success].

NOTES

QUICK START

	I can start this tomorrow	I can begin this month	I need to discuss this with others	Resources needed
Inventory existing formative assessments that will be used during this investigation cycle. Categorize each as short-, medium-, or long-cycle assessments.				
Assess your inventory to identify gaps. These are assessments that do not yield the evidence needed by the PLC+ team to make decisions related to the common challenge.				
Add short-, medium-, and long-cycle assessments that will yield monitoring information.				
Plan the timing of these assessments so the PLC+ team can interpret results and make decisions during specific meetings.				
Determine how results will be shared with key stakeholders, including students and peers.				

Available for download at **https://companion.corwin.com/courses/PLC**

RECIPROCAL PEER OBSERVATIONS

Class teaching can be an isolating act, particularly if you don't get many opportunities to see your colleagues in action. When we visit others, we can see learning in action because we are not focused on delivering instruction and monitoring students. Most teachers report that one of the things they long for in their professional lives is the opportunity to visit each other's classrooms. The benefits of reciprocal peer observations include the following:

- Opportunities to discuss challenges and successes with trusted colleagues
- Support for sharing ideas and expertise among teachers
- Building a community of trust through opening classroom practice to a wider audience (and not just evaluators)
- Self-reflection on the impact of teaching on learning

And yet in practice, relatively few teachers take it upon themselves to actually observe one another. There are some barriers that get in the way, and time is certainly one of them. During a busy school day, it can be easy to put off a visit to a colleague's classroom because of last-minute logistics. Yet the reasons for the hesitation probably run deeper than that. A study of resistance to peer observation by educators found that teachers expressed mild concerns about being the observer, with one person noting that "my presence can make my colleague feel professionally questioned or judged."

Many of the teachers in the study expressed an even stronger resistance to being observed by a peer. Their reasons included the following:

- "I can feel that my professionalism is questioned or judged by a colleague."
- "During the observation, my lesson may not work as I expect or plan."
- "The presence of an observer in the classroom can distract me and/or my students."[81]

One way to address these issues is to arrange for teachers to visit peers who teach different grades or different content.[82] Ideally, relational trust develops on a team, and teachers can visit peers whom they are collaborating with as part of the PLC+.

RECIPROCAL PEER OBSERVATION PROTOCOL TO PROMOTE EXPERT NOTICING

Expert noticing is the ability to integrate the meaning of what is seen, rather than just telling what has been observed. Experts hypothesize and test, elaborate on what they observe, and engage in metacognitive behaviors.[83] This protocol is designed to support expert noticing during reciprocal peer observations. Use the guiding prompts to focus on key instructional elements, describing what you observe without evaluating.

Purpose: To help educators learn to observe and actually notice student learning in real time. In doing so, they consider their own practices, validating what they do and revising their approaches.

Reciprocal Peer Observation Prompts and Notes

Observer's Name:

Teacher Being Observed:

Date and Time of Observation:

Grade Level/Subject Observed:

Focus of Visit: What specific aspect of teaching and learning are both of you focusing on?

Focus Area:

Student Actions: Examples of what to observe:
What are students doing?
- Are they speaking with peers or responding to questions?
- How are they interacting with learning intentions and success criteria?
- How are they interacting with materials, tools, or technology?

What I noticed:

Teacher Moves: Examples of what to observe:
What is the teacher saying or doing during instruction?
- How does the teacher introduce or clarify the learning intention and success criteria?
- What strategies are used to prompt student participation?
- How does the teacher respond to students' questions?

What I noticed:

(Continued)

(Continued)

Interactions:
How are students and the teacher interacting?

Examples of what to observe:
- *What types of questions are being asked (open/closed)?*
- *How are students responding to feedback or direction?*
- *What evidence of collaboration (peer-to-peer or teacher-student) is visible?*

What I noticed:

Environment and Tools:
What aspects of the environment or resources are being used?

Examples of what to observe:
- *What tools/materials are the students using?*
- *How does the physical setup (seating, displays) support learning?*

What I noticed:

Reflective Prompts for the Observer

1. *Patterns:* What repeated strategies or teaching behaviors did I notice?
2. *Surprises:* What surprised me about the instruction?
3. *Connections:* How does what I observed connect to my own teaching practice?
4. *Extension:* What elements of the lesson might I try in my own classroom?

After each teacher has had an opportunity to be both an observer and the person observed, they meet to debrief the experiences and provide feedback to one another.

Reciprocal Peer Observation Debrief Prompts and Notes

Reflective Questions for the Observer to Ask the Observed Teacher

- What aspects of your teaching went well during this lesson?
- Were there any moments where students struggled or were disengaged?

Notes:

Reflective Questions for the Person Observed to Ask the Observer

- What practices did you observe that could inform your own teaching?
- What questions do you have about my strategies?

Notes:

Feedback Framework: Strengths Observed	• e.g., "The use of visuals helped students stay focused and understand the concept." Notes:
Feedback Framework: Questions for Reflection	• e.g., "How might using more wait time encourage broader participation?" Notes:
Feedback Framework: Suggestions for Consideration (if requested)	• e.g., "You could try adding a quick poll to gauge understanding in real time." Notes:
Follow-Up Actions	• What steps will you take as a result of this observation? • How can we continue the conversation to deepen learning? Notes:

Video 4.4
A team works through the Reciprocal
Peer Observation protocol
qrs.ly/1jghoc8

NOTES

QUICK START

	I can start this tomorrow	I can begin this month	I need to discuss this with others	Resources needed
Initiate a conversation about reciprocal peer observation with colleagues.				
Come to consensus about an instructional aspect of the common challenge that we will observe and discuss.				
Determine the logistics and scheduling of the reciprocal observations.				
Prepare students for having other teachers in the classroom by discussing your team's commitment to learn with others.				
Reflect on your comfort level with peer observations. Consider any concerns or reservations you may have about this practice and analyze the underlying reasons for these feelings. How can you address or reframe these thoughts to engage more openly in the process?				

Available for download at **https://companion.corwin.com/courses/PLC**

MICROTEACHING

Seeking feedback is one of the major indicators of students who drive their own learning because this step shows their motivation, critical thinking, and metacognition. Similarly, peer feedback for educators that is gained and provided through microteaching can be an invaluable tool as teams work to refine their professional practice.

Microteaching is the process of recording a short video (no more than five to ten minutes) and using it as a vehicle during team meetings to spur discussion and feedback. In the 1960s, it was developed by the Stanford Teacher Preparation Program as a means for preservice teachers to provide feedback and receive feedback, and it quickly spread to in-service professional learning with experienced teachers.[84]

There are several conditions that can make microteaching a success for your PLC+ team:

1. The teacher to be recorded is a volunteer who decides what they would like to get feedback about.

2. The microteaching is offered in a safe and supportive environment, which involves creating a culture of open communication, collaboration, and constructive feedback.

3. The microteaching is not evaluative.

There are several steps teams can take to ensure the microteaching meets the three main criteria:

- *Use neutral language.* Avoid terms that imply judgment. For instance, say, "I noticed you used open-ended questions" instead of "You did a good job with questioning."

- *Stick to the observable.* Base feedback on what can be seen or heard in the video. For instance, point out, "When you gave students time to think, two more hands went up."

- *Connect feedback to the teacher's focus.* Keep feedback centered on the specific area the volunteer teacher requested.

- *Frame suggestions as possibilities.* Use open-ended questions or exploratory language. For instance, ask, "What do you think would happen if you tried . . . ?"

- *Encourage reflection.* Prompt the volunteer teacher to think deeply about their choices without imposing conclusions. For instance, ask, "What might you do differently if you taught this lesson again?"

NOTES

MICROTEACHING PROTOCOL FOR PLC+ TEAMS

This protocol allows people to explain their thinking and hear the reactions of others. Microteaching focuses on the decisions that teachers make in the act of teaching and allows them to share their mindset, including their beliefs about learning and student engagement.

Purpose: To practice sharing thinking about teaching with others, allowing each member of the team an opportunity to refine their own thinking about actions that improve student learning.

Preparation (Before the Microteaching Session)

1. **Set the Focus:**
   - The volunteer teacher who will be on video identifies a specific teaching skill or strategy they want to analyze (e.g., pacing, questioning techniques, student engagement).
   - The focus should align to the current common challenge.

2. **Select the Segment:**
   - The volunteer teacher records their teaching and chooses a five- to ten-minute segment that reflects the area of focus. This may require that the volunteer teacher watch the video several times to clarify what will be shared.

3. **Share the Segment in Advance:**
   - If possible, share the recording and observation prompts with the team in advance of the team meeting to allow for thoughtful review.
   - Observation prompts might include these:
     - "What evidence of student understanding do you see?"
     - "How are students engaging with the learning?"

4. **Prepare Feedback Roles:**
   - Assign roles to others in the team meeting:
     - *Activator:* Keeps the conversation focused and ensures feedback remains nonevaluative
     - *PLC+ team colleagues:* Focus on the prompts and take notes during the video review

The Microteaching Debrief With the Team

1. **Introduce the Session (5 minutes):**
   - The volunteer teacher provides context for the segment, including these:
     - Framing the lesson, including the learning intention, success criteria, and assessment opportunities
     - The specific teaching focus they want feedback on
     - Any challenges or questions they have about their practice

2. **Watch the Segment Together and Make Observation Notes (5–10 minutes):**
   - The team views the selected recording segment.
   - Observers focus on the observation prompts and take notes without

(Continued)

(Continued)

judgment, describing observable behaviors, strategies, and outcomes (e.g., "Students responded quickly when asked _____ question").

Feedback (After the Video Review)

1. **Volunteer Teacher Reflection (3–5 minutes):**
   - The volunteer teacher shares their perspective on the video segment:
     - What they noticed while rewatching
     - What they felt went well
     - What they want feedback on or what they're curious about

2. **Observer Feedback (5–7 minutes):**
   - Observers share feedback using a structured framework:
     - *Strengths:* Highlight specific examples of effective strategies or actions (e.g., "When you paused after asking a question, students had more time to respond").
     - *Questions:* Pose reflective questions to explore the teacher's thinking or decision-making as it relates to the focus and the common challenge (e.g., "What led you to group students in that way?").
     - *Suggestions:* Offer ideas or alternative strategies framed as possibilities (e.g., "Have you thought about trying _____ next time?").

3. **Group Discussion (3–5 minutes):**
   - Collaboratively discuss patterns, insights, or new strategies as a team.
     - Focus on how feedback applies to broader teaching contexts related to the common challenge.
     - Plan future sessions to revisit the same teaching focus or explore new areas based on team goals.

Quality Checklist for Microteaching

- ☐ Participants see teaching and learning *and* hear the thinking of the volunteer teacher.
- ☐ The discussion is nonevaluative.
- ☐ Team members ask clarifying questions and probes to understand the thinking and mindset of the volunteer teacher.
- ☐ The team decides on strategies or practices to implement and test in classrooms.

Video 4.5
A team works through the Microteaching protocol
qrs.ly/a5ghocc

NOTES

QUICK START

	I can start this tomorrow	I can begin this month	I need to discuss this with others	Resources needed
Learn more about the research behind microteaching.				
If you have not engaged in microteaching before, discuss the benefits of including microteaching in the investigation cycle.				
Practice role-playing a microteaching event using an existing commercially prepared video that spotlights an instructional practice related to your common challenge.				
Come to consensus on a practice and identify a volunteer teacher.				
Model seeking feedback. Inform students that you will be filming a portion of a lesson to gather feedback from other teachers to improve your teaching practice. Demonstrate enthusiasm for being a lifelong learner.				

Available for download at **https://companion.corwin.com/courses/PLC**

CAPACITY-BUILDING LEARNING WALKS

The practice of observing classrooms was traditionally seen as the purview of administrators, whether for evaluation purposes or to gauge progress across a department or a school. Fortunately, the popularity of learning walks has invited teachers into spaces where only administrators once stood. PLC+ learning walks are designed to promote decision-making within teams as members visit at least three classrooms for about ten minutes each. This protocol emphasizes reflection, encourages collaboration, and uses a nonevaluative approach to improve teaching and learning outcomes. Learning walks have been transformative in the schools and districts we work with, especially ensuring that professional learning is implemented into professional practice.[85] When schools adopt learning walks as standard practice, they create a turning point in fostering teacher leadership across the professional learning community.

Learning walks differ from instructional rounds in their scope and their formality.[86] While instructional rounds use protocols for establishing long-term networks, defining problems of practice, and formally analyzing patterns, learning walks are more loosely structured. Here are some key recommendations to help you successfully implement capacity-building learning walks:

- *Focus on equity and fairness.* Observe how instructional strategies impact all students, particularly those who may require additional support.

- *Engage in collaborative reflection.* Use the learning walks as a springboard for collective problem-solving and strategy development, especially in noticing and reflecting.[87]

- *Celebrate successes.* Recognize effective practices observed to promote a positive, growth-oriented culture.

CAPACITY-BUILDING LEARNING WALK PROTOCOL

Classroom learning walks are conducted to gather insights into teaching practices by observing brief snapshots of different classrooms, allowing educators to identify best practices, reflect on their own teaching, and ultimately improve student learning across the school, all while being nonevaluative in nature; this essentially provides a way to learn from each other and collaborate on improving instruction without feeling judged.

Purpose: To collaboratively observe teaching and learning in action, identify practices that support student outcomes, and reflect on strategies to improve collective teacher efficacy.

STEP 1: Preparation (Before the observations)

- **Establish Goals and Focus:**
  - Identify the purpose of the learning walk. Focus areas should be related to the common challenge the team has identified or is in the process of identifying. The observation is a time for the volunteer teachers to profile the area of focus. For instance, if the common challenge concerns collaborative learning, the observed time should coincide with students engaged in collaborative learning.
  - Clearly define observation prompts (e.g., "What strategies promote student participation?").
  - Schedule dates and times with the volunteer teachers on the PLC+ team. Observations should be no more than ten minutes.

- **Set Norms for Observations:**
  - *Nonevaluative:* Observations are descriptive, not judgmental.
  - *Confidential:* All observations and discussions stay within the team.
  - *Focus on Practices, Not Individuals:* Observations are about student learning and instructional strategies, not teacher performance.

- **Assign Roles:**
  - *Observers:* Teachers who observe the classrooms.
  - *Activator:* Keeps the team focused on the goals and manages the post-observation discussion.
  - *Timekeeper:* Ensures the group stays on schedule.

- **Context Briefing (5 minutes):**
  - The host teacher briefly introduces the lesson:
    - What is the learning intention and success criteria?
    - What strategies or practices should observers focus on?
    - Are there any specific areas where feedback is welcome?

(Continued)

(Continued)

Step 2: Observation (During the learning walk)

- **Classroom Observation (10 minutes):**
  - Observers enter the classroom quietly, staying unobtrusive.
  - Observe and take notes aligned with the focus prompts, not other extraneous information unrelated to the agreed focus.
- **Descriptive Note-Taking:**
  - Observers record what they see and hear without making judgments (e.g., "Three students are using manipulatives to solve problems," not "The students look engaged").
  - **Repeat in at least two more classrooms to identify trends and patterns.**

STEP 3: Debrief and Reflection (Either immediately after the observation or at the next PLC+ team meeting)

- **Reflect (5–7 minutes):**
  - Observers take 1–2 minutes to individually review and organize their notes.
  - Reflect on:
    - Patterns or trends observed
    - Any surprises or questions raised during the observation
- **Team Discussion (15–20 minutes):**
  - Use a structured framework for sharing observations:
    - *Description:* Share observable evidence as it relates to the agreed focus (e.g., "All three teachers posed an open-ended question, and at least three students in each class responded verbally").
    - *Analysis:* Discuss what the observations suggest about learning and teaching as it relates to the common challenge (e.g., "Open-ended questions seem to increase participation").
    - *Application:* Brainstorm ideas for implementing similar practices to address the common challenge (e.g., "How can we use open-ended questions in our lessons?").

STEP 4: Reflect on the Process (5–10 minutes):

- As a team, discuss the learning walk:
  - What did the team learn from the observation?
  - How can these insights inform our practice?
  - Were the observation prompts effective? (Revise protocol as needed for next time.)

Quality Checklist for Capacity-Building Learning Walks

- ☐ The common challenge drives the focus of the learning walk.
- ☐ The discussion is non-evaluative.
- ☐ Trends and pattens are noted and analyzed.
- ☐ The team decides on strategies or practices to implement and test in classrooms.

Video 4.6
A team works through the Capacity-Building Learning Walks protocol
qrs.ly/v2ghoci

QUICK START

	I can start this tomorrow	I can begin this month	I need to discuss this with others	Resources needed
Learn about your school district's experiences with learning walks, as there may be an existing protocol already in use.				
Identify an agreed area of focus for the learning walk.				
Schedule a time when members can participate.				
Discuss the observations and what you can implement from the experience.				
Write notes of thanks to your colleagues for hosting you in their classroom for the learning walk.				

Available for download at https://companion.corwin.com/courses/PLC

LEARNING FROM FOCAL STUDENTS

As we have noted, focal students represent specific learners whose progress can illuminate broader patterns of success or challenges within a classroom or school. These students can inform educators about their learning. And the evidence collected from focal students can be analyzed for trends that can be applied to more students. By focusing on a few representative students, PLC teams can dive deeply into data, tailor instructional strategies, and monitor the impact of their efforts.[88] This approach aligns with crosscutting PLC+ values, particularly equity and collective efficacy, by keeping the diverse needs of all students at the forefront of decision-making.

The importance of focal students lies in their ability to provide insights that extend beyond their individual experiences. For example, choosing students who represent varying achievement levels, linguistic backgrounds, or social-emotional needs can help teams better understand how instructional, curricular, and assessment decisions affect different groups of learners. This practice prevents generalizations and ensures that the team's discussions and actions are grounded in real, observable evidence. Furthermore, the inclusion of focal students encourages accountability; teams can track specific interventions and assess their outcomes, fostering high expectations and a shared sense of responsibility for student success.

To select focal students, teams should first identify the goals of their investigation. For instance, if the focus is on improving literacy outcomes, then they might select students with a range of reading abilities, including a high performer, a struggling reader, and a multilingual learner. Teams should rely on a combination of short-, medium-, and long-cycle quantitative data and qualitative observations to choose students who reflect key patterns in the broader class. It's also crucial to rotate focal students periodically, especially for each new investigation cycle, to ensure that the team examines a variety of perspectives and remains inclusive.

Once the focal students are selected, the PLC+ team should develop a detailed plan for tracking each focal student's progress. This includes setting measurable goals, identifying evidence-based strategies, and establishing timelines for review. Protocols, such as analyzing student work or conducting peer observations, can help teams systematically examine the impact of their efforts. By keeping focal students at the center of their conversations, teams can drive meaningful improvements in teaching and learning while reinforcing their commitment to collective action.

ASK A BOT

Bots can quickly analyze student work samples and identify strengths and next-steps learning. As with other AI-generated responses, teachers and teams need to review the output for accuracy, but having this output can jumpstart the team into action. Specifically, as teams review the bot's analysis of the focal students' performance, they can identify trends across their classes and decide what they need to teach all of the students versus some of the students. Here's a sample prompt for analyzing student work:

> This is the assessment information from a _____ grade student learning the following content **[INSERT STANDARDS OR LEARNING INTENTIONS]**. The success criteria [or grading rubric] for this assignment [or assessment] is: **[INSERT CRITERIA]**. Please identify the strengths that this student demonstrates and at least two areas of next-steps learning.

NOTES

QUICK START

	I can start this tomorrow	I can begin this month	I need to discuss this with others	Resources needed
Look for students who represent different levels of achievement (high-performing, struggling, and average learners).				
Consider disaggregated data to ensure student representation, such as multilingual learners, students with disabilities, and students from different demographic backgrounds.				
Select students who might typically be overlooked in broader analyses, such as those with inconsistent attendance, quiet personalities, or unrecognized potential.				
Ask, "Who are we not talking about?" or "Whose voice is missing in our data?"				
Rotate focal students in other investigation cycles to ensure that insights reflect a range of perspectives.				

Available for download at **https://companion.corwin.com/courses/PLC**

CASE IN POINT: PRIVATE PRACTICE

Teachers in intermediate grades at Jefferson Elementary sat in a circle in their school's library, the usual chatter subdued. They were focused on their common challenge—how to better support their multilingual learners in using academic language. Despite weeks of brainstorming strategies, they hadn't made much progress. The real issue was unspoken: No one wanted to open their classroom for observation. They had never engaged in learning walks.

Third-grade teacher Melody Daniels broke the silence. "I feel like we're stuck. We've shared a lot of ideas, but I'm not sure we're getting to the root of what's happening in our classrooms."

Darius Carter, a fifth-grade teacher, nodded. "I think you're right. I'd love to see how some of these strategies actually work, but inviting people into my room feels intimidating."

"I get it," added third-grade teacher Valeria Rivera. "It's hard not to feel like it's a performance. But we're all here to help each other, right? We're not trying to judge."

Melody leaned forward. "What if we start small? We've been talking about using juicy sentences[89] to focus on syntax and vocabulary. But we're all struggling to implement it. We could invite each other to observe a short part of the lesson—maybe a few minutes. Then we could focus on how the multilingual students respond."

Darius hesitated, then smiled. "I'll try it. I think that could be really helpful."

The team agreed, and for the first time in weeks, the tension in the room eased.

What's Your Advice?

- Melody and Darius both served as activators, getting the team to engage in critical dialogue. But now they need help in figuring out how to get started. What advice do you have for them? What are mistakes they should avoid?

- This team has been reluctant to open their doors to one another, suggesting there may be some issues with trust even though they are pleasant to one another. How can trust be built among a team that gets along well enough but hasn't had much experience at collaborating in meaningful ways?

Video 4.7
An activator reflects on the case in point
qrs.ly/e5ghock

CROSSCUTTING VALUES CHECK

How does your team prototype and try new approaches, and how does your team learn together? How often do you talk about what you, and your students, are learning? Consider these reflective questions to spark discussion with colleagues.

Equity and Fairness

- Do we have a process to ensure that every member is both an observer and one who is observed by colleagues?
- Do we utilize a range of quantitative and qualitative short-, medium-, and long-cycle formative assessments?
- Do we consult our students about their perspectives on what we prototype and try?

High Expectations

- Do our expectations for collegial trust building extend to all teachers, from novice to experienced to expert, or are they reserved only for new teachers in a formal induction program?
- Do we hold ourselves accountable for engaging in practices such as learning walks, reciprocal peer observations, and microteaching?
- In what ways do we demonstrate high expectations for ourselves by ensuring we identify a range of focal students to monitor our decisions?

Individual and Collective Efficacy

- Do we engage in critical dialogue?
- Do we innovate and take risks in our teaching?
- Do we have a shared responsibility for all the students in our school, not just those on our own roster? What opportunities exist to share across teams and learn from others?

Activators

- Do we honor this phase of the investigation cycle by making our own learning a priority?
- In what ways do we have evidence of how we activate each other's thinking?
- Do we demonstrate a willingness to challenge each other's thinking in ways that are kind and growth-producing?

SELF-ASSESSMENT

To answer the question "What did we learn today?" teams must look for evidence of learning, reflect on both aggregated and disaggregated evidence of learning, and then take action based upon the evidence available. Again, moving forward may require the PLC+ team to further their own professional learning, to simply change their approach to teaching this particular skill or content, or to implement a combination of the two approaches. Answers to this question also provide the team with a clear understanding of who did—and did not—benefit from instruction, which we will explore further in Module 5.

Rapid Assessment:

We regularly examine our practice, discuss expectations, identify and act on student needs, and seek to describe elements of our practice that yield—or do not yield—a measurable, positive impact.

1	2	3	4	5
Not Begun or Not Initiated	Very Limited Evidence of Capacity	Some Evidence of Capacity	Evidence of Capacity and Limited Evidence of Effective Implementation	Evidence of Capacity and Demonstrated Effective Implementation

Queries for Conducting a Detailed Assessment:

	What Did We Learn Today?	Not Begun or Not Initiated	Very Limited Evidence of Capacity	Some Evidence of Capacity	Evidence of Capacity and Limited Evidence of Effective Implementation	Evidence of Capacity and Demonstrated Effective Implementation
4.1	We can describe, with evidence, elements of our practice that are—and are not—yielding an impact.	1	2	3	4	5
4.2	We regularly discuss the expectations we have for our students, including identifying areas of consensus and lack of consensus across our team.	1	2	3	4	5
4.3	Our reflections on practice regularly lead to new actions or changes to previously defined actions.	1	2	3	4	5
4.4	Our work makes a distinction between student progress and student achievement, attending to each in effective ways.	1	2	3	4	5
4.5	We engage in professional learning through microteaching and capacity-building learning walks.	1	2	3	4	5

 Available for download at https://companion.corwin.com/courses/PLC

NOTICE AND REFLECT

 **ESSENTIAL QUESTION**

How do we learn about our efforts to impact student learning and share that with others?

THINK ABOUT

- Do we have a school culture of being in each other's classrooms for the purpose of learning ourselves?
- Do we engage in critical dialogue about school or team initiatives?
- Do we have a shared responsibility for the learning of all of the students in the school and all of the adults in the school?

START – STOP – KEEP

Based on what you learned in this module, answer the questions below.

Start: What practice(s) would you like to start doing?
Stop: What practice(s) would you like to stop doing?
Keep: What practice(s) would you like to keep doing?

NOTES

5 WHO BENEFITED AND WHO DID NOT?

The question that is the focus of this module, "Who benefited and who did not?" is central to the PLC+ model because it places benefit at the forefront of teaching and learning. In any educational initiative, it's easy to focus solely on aggregate data, celebrating successes without fully interrogating which students those successes include—or exclude. It has become too common for schools to accept that certain students, because of their demographic, language, or ability profiles, will not make progress. To combat that stance, the focus question forces teams to dig deeper, ensuring that their practices are not just effective in general but equitable in their impact. By prioritizing this inquiry, educators confront disparities and recognize patterns of inequity that might otherwise remain hidden, aligning with the PLC+ commitment to equitable outcomes for all learners.

A Liberatory Design approach aligns intentions with actions by creating a space for teams to embrace the messiness and complexity of the challenge that occurs in any effective change process. Embracing the messiness and complexity allows teams to enlist the insights of others, including students and families. Teams that cling to a naïve assumption that linear plans will unfold exactly as expected undermine their own wisdom and creativity.

Let's take another look at the Liberatory Design thinking illustration.

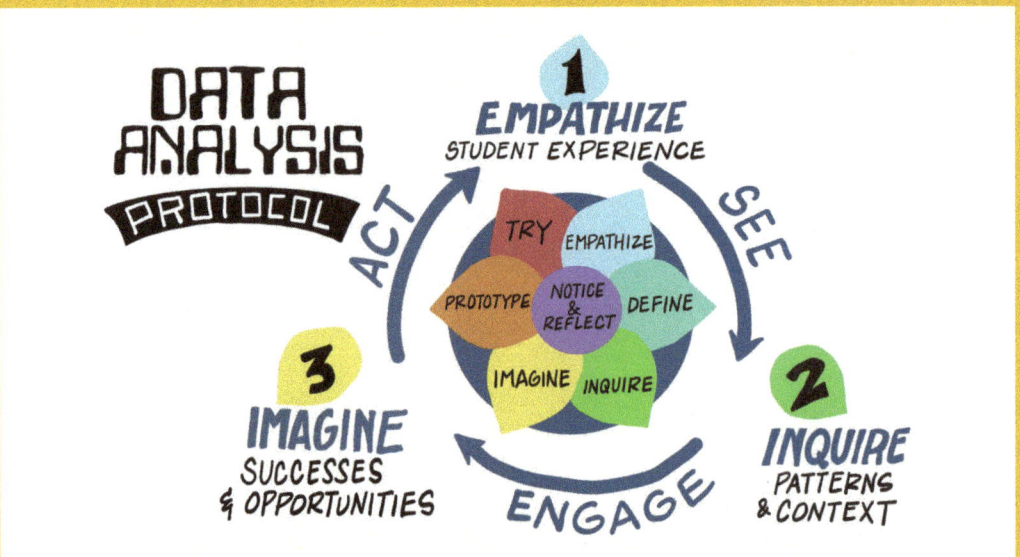

Adapted from "Liberatory Design for Equity" by the National Equity Project. Derived from Anaissie, T., Cary, V., Clifford, D., Malarkey, T. & Wise, S. (2021). Liberatory Design. www.liberatorydesign.com.

This time we shall focus on the cyclical nature of design inquiry, which is See-Engage-Act:[90]

- SEE: See and understand the territory you're navigating.
- ENGAGE: Engage others to make meaning of your current situation.
- ACT: Take action to address your challenge—and learn from that action.

The work of PLC+ teams is not decontextualized, which is why the See-Engage-Act heuristic is so important; it captures the decision-making techniques we use as humans to find satisfactory solutions when conditions are less than optimal (which pretty much describes any classroom or school). Using this process, teams consider the contexts in which learning occurs, including individual and environmental factors, and they identify any structural or institutional barriers that may be hiding in plain sight. The ultimate purpose of these steps is to take action with confidence based on the systems that impact student and teacher learning.

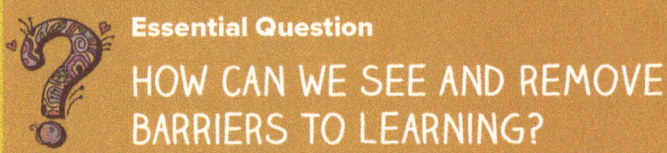

Essential Question

HOW CAN WE SEE AND REMOVE BARRIERS TO LEARNING?

Video 5.1
An elementary team discusses question 5
qrs.ly/sxghocl

Video 5.2
A secondary team discusses question 5
qrs.ly/94ghocm

TWO TRUTHS AND A LIE

*Two of these statements are true; one is false.
Can you spot the lie?*

1. A chief purpose of a PLC is to identify students for intervention.

2. Data-use efforts by teams that have an explicit focus on equity are more likely to lead to school policies and practices that expand students' opportunities to learn, whereas efforts that lack this explicit focus run the risk of limiting students' learning trajectories.

3. A lack of shared vision at the onset of a team's work in a professional learning community can negatively impact the team's ability to work with the data it gathers in making meaningful decisions.

We'll start off with the false statement, which is the first one: The role of professional learning communities is not to identify students in need of intervention. In fact, our experiences have shown that when PLC teams default to MTSS efforts for any student who did not master content, their shared responsibility is diminished. Without intending to, they distance themselves and instead allow others to shoulder the work. In fact, in a scoping review of seventy-nine studies of PLCs with an MTSS focus, there was virtually no evidence that classroom teachers applied intervention approaches in their classrooms.[91] We question where the learning actually occurs when there is no change in professional practice.

The second statement is true. When teams design and implement common challenges that focus on equity, schools create new policies and practices that increase students' opportunities to learn. In a study of eight elementary, middle, and high schools in four districts, schools that used an equity lens in their PLCs used their data to challenge assumptions, expand flexible grouping, and maintain focus on all students. Those that did not apply an equity lens focused instead on administrative compliance, increased tracking, and narrowed their attention to students who were "on the bubble"—students posed to move into the next level of achievement and thereby affect the school's test scores.[92]

Unfortunately, the third statement is also true. In a study of failed professional learning communities in the US and the Netherlands, a common throughline was a lack of a shared vision. This manifested itself when teams reviewed data, causing tension, agitation, and hostility within the teams and directed at others in the school as well.[93] Because the teams didn't agree on what the problem was at the outset, they devolved into disarray as the weeks went on and were unable to make consequential decisions. One teacher in the study summarized their data (mis)use this way: "We basically look at what standards the students are not getting, and then that's about it. So we identify the issue, but we don't find the solution, so then we go back to our classrooms, and hopefully we're all finding the solution."

We want your experience to be different. Your wisdom is consequential, and your decisions should be, too.

THE STORY BEHIND THE QUESTION (WHO BENEFITTED AND WHO DID NOT?)

In *Schools That Learn*, Peter Senge applied the principles of organizational learning from his earlier work, *The Fifth Discipline*, to the educational context. He emphasized that schools must operate as dynamic learning organizations where all stakeholders—teachers, administrators, students, and the broader community—engage in continuous learning and improvement. A key idea is that schools are interconnected systems, and addressing complex challenges requires seeing the larger patterns and leveraging collective expertise to create sustainable change.[94]

Like Senge's framework, PLC+ emphasizes the importance of collective efficacy, team learning, and systems thinking. PLC+ also requires that teams uncover patterns in the data. Past PLC models did not focus on trend data, but rather on individual students. However, it's not sufficient to identify individual students who did not learn as expected and then send them to intervention. Instead, there are patterns that emerge, often hiding in plain sight, that teams must uncover to deliver on the promise of equity and ensure that their school systems are fair.

Both Senge's framework and PLC+ advocate for reflective practices and collaboration to achieve shared goals. For example, Senge's concept of mental models—challenging assumptions and aligning perspectives—parallels the PLC+ focus on Liberatory Design while fostering equity, inclusivity, and a shared understanding of student needs. Additionally, the value placed on shared vision in both frameworks underscores the necessity of aligning team goals with the larger mission of improving student outcomes.

Video 5.3
Nancy discusses the story behind question 5
qrs.ly/arghocn

By asking about benefit, especially differential benefit for some students, members are moved to take action and increase their impact. The approach requires teams to actively seek solutions for students who are not yet succeeding and to implement those solutions with urgency. This cycle of reflection and action also ensures that improvement efforts are not static but dynamic, evolving to meet the diverse and changing needs of students. By continually asking, "Who benefited and who did not?" PLC+ teams maintain a laser focus on the ultimate goal of education: fostering growth and achievement for every learner, regardless of background or circumstance. This key question, while simple, drives the transformative work necessary to achieve that vision.

DETERMINING IMPACT THROUGH INITIAL AND END-OF-UNIT ASSESSMENTS

Performance assessments are a critical component for determining who benefited and who did not. One of the easiest ways to make these determinations is to gauge progress across the investigative cycle using initial and end-of-unit assessments. Conventional formats allow students to demonstrate their knowledge and skills; these are typically aligned with success criteria for the unit and are intended to align to the common challenge. The goal for teachers is to use these assessments to gain insight into their students' ability to apply what they have learned.

Each assessment type has its benefits and cautions, as no single assessment can provide all the information needed (see Figure 5.1). A mix of item types can be useful and efficient and provide a richer picture of progress over time. However, a barrier to rich PLC+ discussions is the narrow view that everyone must universally use the exact items. This misconception prevents the formation of teams that span grade levels or content areas. Rather, teams should identify assessment tasks that serve as sentinels for measuring the impact of an investigation. For example, a team of teachers from multiple grade levels who are focused on vocabulary development will naturally provide instruction on different words and phrases tailored to each grade level; to assess how well this instruction is working, each member can identify the specific terms they will be monitoring and include items on the initial and end-of-unit measures.

Figure 5.1 • Benefits and Cautions for Assessment Types

Assessment Type	Benefits	Cautions
Multiple-Choice Questions	• Efficient for assessing a broad range of content quickly • Easy to grade • Can assess factual knowledge, comprehension, and some application skills	• Often focus on lower-level cognitive skills like recall • Poor distractors may lead to guessing • Limited in assessing higher-order thinking • Can favor test-taking strategies over understanding
Short Constructed Responses	• Require students to generate their own answers, encouraging critical thinking • Allow teachers to evaluate reasoning and understanding in a concise format • Are useful for explaining concepts or solving problems	• Scoring can be subjective unless clear rubrics are used • May not provide enough space for students to elaborate on complex ideas • Time-intensive for teachers to grade, especially in large classes
Extended Constructed Responses	• Encourage deep thinking, analysis, and synthesis of ideas • Allow students to connect multiple concepts and articulate reasoning • Align well with standards emphasizing critical thinking and problem-solving	• Require significant time to complete and grade • May disadvantage students with weak writing skills unrelated to content knowledge • Subjective grading risks unless robust rubrics are used
Essay Responses	• Assess comprehensive understanding and the ability to develop arguments • Support creativity and originality • Ideal for evaluating higher-order thinking like evaluation and synthesis	• Highly time-consuming for both students and teachers • Grading is inherently more subjective, even with rubrics • May disadvantage multilingual learners or students with writing disabilities
Problem-Solving Tasks	• Emphasize application of knowledge to real-world situations • Develop students' critical thinking and reasoning • Suitable for assessing procedural fluency and conceptual understanding	• Require careful construction to ensure problems are neither too simple nor overly complex • Can frustrate students if poorly scaffolded • Scoring consistency can be challenging, especially for multistep problems
Performance Tasks With Rubrics	• Assess practical skills and creativity • Provide a clear and transparent evaluation framework for students • Encourage engagement through hands-on activities	• Developing quality rubrics can be time-intensive • Can be resource-intensive in terms of materials and class time • Students unfamiliar with performance tasks may need additional support to succeed

(Continued)

(Continued)

Assessment Type	Benefits	Cautions
Oral or Visual Presentations	• Assess communication, collaboration, and presentation skills alongside content knowledge • Promote student creativity and engagement • Offer opportunities for peer and self-assessment	• May favor students who are confident speakers or visually creative • Time-consuming for large classes, as each presentation takes time • Grading can be subjective without detailed rubrics

ASK A BOT

Use a chatbot to help your team identify sentinel items that represent the common challenge your team is investigating. Develop a prompt that takes into account the focus of the unit and the specific nature of the common challenge the team is investigating. Here's an example:

> Our team is interested in designing items that can be used for an initial assessment and then later at the end of the unit. The lessons focus on **[INSERT THE FOCUS, FOR EXAMPLE, IMPROVING NUMBER SENSE]** with students in **[IDENTIFY GRADE, FOR EXAMPLE, THIRD AND FOURTH GRADE]**. Please develop **[NUMBER OF]** assessment items (or tasks) that include a range of cognitive complexity.

When the team has assessment items or tasks to consider, they can discuss the following:

- Does the task or identified item(s) explicitly require students to demonstrate knowledge related to our common challenge?
- Does the task or identified item(s) draw on a variety of formats?
- Does the task or identified item(s) focus on student strengths and assets, not just reveal their weaknesses?
- Are the instructions clear enough for students?
- Is the assessment accessible to all students, including multilingual learners and those with disabilities?
- Does the rubric or criteria for success align with the proposed items?

QUICK START

	I can start this tomorrow	I can begin this month	I need to discuss this with others	Resources needed
Examine current assessments to identify possible items or tasks you might use. What are the benefits and barriers to the tools that your team is currently using to collect evidence of student learning?				
Consult with special educators and language specialists about mistakes to avoid or techniques to use when designing an assessment.				
Consider your own assessment literacy and identify resources that can strengthen your approach.				
Use a chatbot to draft initial assessment items or tasks for your team to consider for initial and end-of-unit comparisons. Consider meeting with focal students to determine the answer to this question: Are the instructions clear enough for students?				
Reflect on the types of assessments you most frequently use and consider how they align with your instructional goals.				
Think about areas where you could expand your repertoire of assessments.				

Available for download at https://companion.corwin.com/courses/PLC

DETERMINE PROGRESS AND ACHIEVEMENT

Video 5.4
Visible Learning Progress and Achievement Tool
qrs.ly/qgghoco

Graphically displaying data can be a powerful way to interpret data generated by the agreed-upon measures that were determined by the team. But too often, the only metric used is whether a student achieved mastery (or did not). This one-dimensional view fails to alert the team to the successes hiding in plain sight—that is, the students who made accelerated progress but who have not yet reached mastery. Do you realize how valuable this information is to the team? It is not only a cause for celebration, but also evidence of what is working (and, therefore, what should be refined and continued).

There is another group that goes unseen in a one-dimensional evidence model: students who were already at or near mastery at the onset and failed to make much progress. They lull teams into a false sense of success, believing that their instruction—and not what students already knew—was the cause. This information is equally valuable, because it causes teams to look more closely at ineffective instructional practices that actually hinder the progress of advanced learners.

A more sophisticated way of analyzing impact is to map data using two variables: progress and achievement. These are gauged based on the initial assessment and the end-of-unit results.

The Visible Learning Progress and Achievement Tool provides teams with a way to visualize the data in terms of both progress and achievement. The QR code will allow you to download an Excel spreadsheet for your PLC+ team to use to make these calculations. Notice that there are tabs for thirty, fifty, and one hundred students. Enter each student's data, including both initial- and post-assessment information. The system will calculate the effect size for each student and the whole group. The system will also calculate the average achievement for the cohort and then plot students in the appropriate quadrant. The resulting progress measure is an effect size, providing you with quantitative information about impact, thus yielding a portrait of who benefited and who did not.

Once the team has mapped student results on progress and achievement, it can engage in preliminary discussion of the findings:

- Based on the effect size data, with which group(s) of students were you most effective? With which group(s) were you least effective? What insights does this provide?
- Were there students who demonstrated progress but did not meet the expected level of achievement?
- How did your focal students perform?
- What preliminary conclusions can you draw from your data analysis regarding student performance and instructional impact?

GOING DEEPER: LOCATING TRENDS AND PATTERNS FOR INDIVIDUAL, ENVIRONMENTAL, AND TEACHING FACTORS

Module 5: Who Benefited and Who Did Not?

As teams look at a performance map, they may realize that the students identified in each of the four quadrants are actually similar in one or more ways. It is essential for teams to analyze patterns or trends in student data for a few reasons.

- Patterns and trends provide insights into the collective learning needs.
- They help teams identify systemic challenges or areas of success.

By focusing on trends, teams can move beyond addressing isolated instances and instead target strategies that benefit larger groups of students. This broader perspective enables teachers to tailor instruction effectively, allocate resources equitably, and implement interventions that address the root causes of student difficulties. Additionally, recognizing trends can help teams align their practices with curriculum standards, assess the effectiveness of teaching strategies, and support professional learning conversations within their professional learning community.

Figure 5.2 • Factors That Can Influence Trends and Patterns

Individual Student Factors	**Attendance Issues** (e.g., chronic absenteeism or tardiness)
	Disabilities (e.g., learning disabilities, autism, intellectual disabilities)
	Language Learning Challenges (e.g., multilingual learners)
	Health Problems (e.g., chronic illnesses; mental health issues, like anxiety or depression)
	Motivation and Engagement (e.g., lack of interest in subject matter, fear or mistrust)
	Prior Knowledge Gaps (e.g., foundational skills missing from earlier grades)
	Behavioral Challenges (e.g., disruptive behavior, low self-regulation skills)
	Home Environment (e.g., lack of access to a quiet space for studying or family support)
	Trauma or Stress (e.g., adverse childhood experiences or family instability)
Environmental Factors	**Socioeconomic Status** (e.g., lack of resources, such as technology or school supplies)
	Transience or Mobility (e.g., joining the class later in the year, interrupted schooling)
	School Climate (e.g., lack of a positive or inclusive learning environment)
	Peer Relationships (e.g., bullying, lack of supportive peer connections)
	Cultural Disconnect (e.g., curriculum or instruction that doesn't reflect students' backgrounds)
Teaching Factors	**Understanding of rigor** (e.g., misjudging the level of cognitive complexity in the standard)
	Preconceived notions of students' abilities (e.g., teacher expectations and beliefs about the potential of some students)
	Data rich, information poor (e.g., collecting a lot of data but not effectively analyzing and interpreting it to gain meaningful insights and then planning actions based on the information)
	Mismatch of instructional materials (e.g., texts, tasks, and assignments not aligned with the learning expectations)

As teams look closely at trends and patterns as these relate to individual and environmental factors, they can extend the discussion by asking these questions:

- What stands out in these data?
- Are there outliers or unexpected trends?
- How do these patterns connect to instructional practices?
- What types of progress and achievement patterns are evident in each quadrant? What factors might have contributed to these outcomes?
- What affordances may have positively contributed to the growth of students who made progress but did not reach mastery?
- Did some students achieve mastery on the post-assessment but show little to no growth compared to their initial assessment? What patterns or factors might explain this?

NOTES

QUICK START

	I can start this tomorrow	I can begin this month	I need to discuss this with others	Resources needed
Use tools such as attendance records, language proficiency scores, and behavioral notes to identify contributing factors for each group. Identify the key student groups you will focus on when analyzing patterns and trends in the data. Consider factors such as gender, language proficiency, special education needs, socioeconomic status, or other relevant characteristics that might reveal important insights about learning outcomes and equity.				
Collaborate with interventionists, special education staff, or multilingual learner specialists to address factors like disabilities or language barriers. Use the QR code to download the Excel spreadsheet, and then populate it with student names to set up for your first entry of student scores.				
Gather or request additional data (e.g., family engagement surveys, health information) to understand environmental influences better. Use the progress and achievement mapping tool in the QR code to analyze pre- and post-assessment data, including calculating effect sizes.				

Available for download at **https://companion.corwin.com/courses/PLC**

EXAMINING COGNITIVE BARRIERS TO IDENTIFY INSTRUCTIONAL FACTORS

Cognitive barriers are obstacles that prevent effective teaching and learning by disrupting how students and teachers interact with knowledge.[95] These barriers stem from a variety of factors, including mental mindsets, insufficient prior knowledge, misconceptions, or ineffective learning strategies. For instance, a student who lacks confidence in their ability to learn may not see the value in engaging with a subject. Similarly, a teacher might struggle to address deeply ingrained misconceptions that students bring into the classroom. As these examples show, cognitive barriers are not just about student deficits—they also represent challenges for educators to overcome by tailoring their strategies to align with specific learning obstacles.

Studies of the complex interplay between students' cognitive barriers and the teacher's instruction indicate that nine cognitive barriers can interfere with learning (see Figure 5.3).

Figure 5.3 • Cognitive Barriers to Learning

Challenge	Description
1. Student mental mindset	• Students hold attitudes and beliefs about a course or topic, such as how interesting or valuable it will be and how capable they are to master it through their own efforts. • Students may believe a course is irrelevant to them or that they lack the ability needed to learn the content.
2. Metacognition and self-regulation	• Students monitor and judge their level of understanding of concepts, and they regulate their learning behaviors to achieve a desired level of mastery. • Students may be overconfident in their level of understanding.
3. Student fear and mistrust	• Students come to a course with a certain level of fear of taking it. Students may interpret the teacher's behavior as being unfair or unsupportive of their learning, resulting in a certain degree of mistrust. • Negative emotional reactions, such as fear or lack of trust in the teacher, can undermine motivation and interfere with learning.

(Continued)

(Continued)

Challenge	Description
4. Insufficient prior knowledge	• Students vary in how much they know about course content at the start of the course. • Some students may have little to no knowledge about the content, putting them at a disadvantage compared to students with a strong background.
5. Misconceptions	• Students often hold faulty or mistaken beliefs about the course content at the start of the course. • Students may cling to misconceptions even when they are taught accurate information.
6. Ineffective learning strategies	• Students can employ various methods to learn course concepts, and these methods vary widely in effectiveness and efficiency. • Students often prefer the least effective learning strategies.
7. Transfer of learning	• Students can vary in their ability and propensity to apply course concepts appropriately outside the classroom context. • Students often fail to apply knowledge beyond the end of a course.
8. Constraints of selective attention	• Students can focus their awareness on only a limited portion of the environment, missing anything outside that focus. • People mistakenly believe they can multitask, switching attention back and forth among different tasks.
9. Constraints of mental effort and working memory	• Students have two major limitations in cognitive processing: the amount of mental effort or concentration available to them and the ability to hold information consciously. • Students are easily overwhelmed by trying to concentrate on too complex a task or to remember too much information.

Source: The cognitive challenges of effective teaching, Stephen L. Chew, William J. Cerbin, *The Journal of Economic Education*, 2020, Taylor & Francis, reprinted by permission of the publisher (Taylor & Francis Ltd, http://www.tandfonline.com).

As a team, examine the two quadrants of the achievement/progress map that identify students who did not make progress, as they did not benefit from instruction. Consider the cognitive barriers these individuals may have faced. Any focal students you previously identified and who fall into these two quadrants should be the first ones to examine. Use the discussion questions in Figure 5.4 to spark reflection and identify preliminary actions for future units.

NOTES

Figure 5.4 • Discussion Questions for Addressing Cognitive Barriers

Cognitive Barrier	Discussion Questions
Student Mindset	What instructional approaches did we use to demonstrate the relevance of our subject matter to students' lives and goals? How do we create opportunities for students to experience success and build confidence?
Fear and Mistrust	How do we communicate fairness and support to students who might distrust the educational system or our intentions? What specific strategies could help create a more emotionally safe learning environment?
Prior Knowledge and Misconceptions	What formative assessments did we use to uncover gaps in prior knowledge or identify misconceptions early? How can we help students unlearn faulty beliefs while building accurate understanding?
Ineffective Learning Strategies	What common learning strategies do our students currently use, and how effective are these methods? Did we explicitly teach and model more effective learning strategies, such as retrieval practice or elaboration? How did we encourage students to reflect on and adjust their learning strategies for better outcomes?
Metacognition and Self-regulation	What evidence do we see of students being overconfident or underconfident in their understanding? What strategies did we teach students to improve their self-assessment of understanding?
Transfer of Learning	How did we evaluate whether students are applying their learning in new and varied contexts? What types of tasks or projects did we design to encourage students to apply their learning beyond the classroom?
Attention and Working Memory	Are our lessons designed to minimize distractions and focus students' attention on the key concepts? How did we break down information into manageable chunks to avoid overwhelming working memory?

Understanding and addressing cognitive barriers requires a proactive, intentional approach. By focusing on the root causes of disengagement rather than on outward behaviors, teachers can increase the precision of their instruction and better support all learners in overcoming obstacles to success.

NOTES

QUICK START

	I can start this tomorrow	I can begin this month	I need to discuss this with others	Resources needed
Discuss the cognitive barriers and the ways that you might identify students experiencing those barriers.				
Identify the cognitive barriers that appear to be prevalent in your classroom, based on student performance or feedback. Are the barriers prevalent enough to become a common challenge in the next cycle?				
Look for specific focal students who are affected by particular cognitive barriers.				
Identify additional actions you can take to address the cognitive barriers that your students experience.				
Consider how instruction, classroom environment, or curriculum design might unintentionally reinforce some of these barriers.				

Available for download at **https://companion.corwin.com/courses/PLC**

CHECKING IN WITH FOCAL STUDENTS

As we have discussed, gathering information from focal students is an invaluable practice for understanding the student experience and for making meaningful adjustments to instruction. These students often represent diverse perspectives within the classroom, providing insights into how teaching strategies, classroom dynamics, and learning environments affect individual engagement and achievement. When teams trust that students have the capacity to be attuned to their own needs, we give learners a voice. Then, by working with these students, we can identify barriers to learning—such as unclear instructions, social dynamics in group work, or unengaging activities—that might otherwise go unnoticed.

Another benefit to all of the participants is that this process fosters a sense of inclusion and respect, as students feel heard and valued in shaping their educational journey. Listening to focal students not only helps us address immediate challenges but also informs our long-term strategies for creating an equitable and effective classroom environment. In keeping with Liberatory Design principles, the process involves gaining insight from stakeholders closest to the challenge—our students—to seek liberatory collaboration by designing with, not for.[96]

It is also important that teams intentionally use the Liberatory Design mindset identified as *recognize oppression* when they analyze data. Let's look at a few examples:

- As the team probes deeper to understand factors contributing to student confusion, they notice that learners from certain cultural groups have expressed more confusion than students from other cultural groups. In response, the teachers decide to implement more culturally responsive approaches to better connect with students whose cultural backgrounds are not the dominant one.

- As the team leans into the mode of *inquire* to explore how students' feelings of agency relate to a lack of voice in group settings, they discover that classroom structures are privileging more extraverted students. They decide to shift the power dynamics as they plan for group collaboration in the classroom.

Unless teams are looking for these types of dynamics, they are likely to escape detection. Yet these types of insights are necessary for teams to identify and meet the needs of underrepresented or underserved populations, ensuring that all students, regardless of background, can thrive academically and socially. By leveraging the authentic perspectives of focal students and working to recognize oppression, teams can make strategic changes that enhance both teaching effectiveness and student outcomes.

To successfully implement this process, teams should gather and analyze student input. Short interviews or surveys work well, depending on the time available and the depth of feedback needed. Questions should be concise, developmentally appropriate, and targeted at areas like clarity of instruction, classroom climate, and preferred learning activities. It's essential to use open-ended prompts to capture nuanced perspectives while including scaled questions for patterns and trends. Figure 5.5 includes some suggestions.

Figure 5.5 • Sample Focal Student Interview Questions

Possible Interview Questions

1. Can you describe a time in class during the last few weeks when you felt very successful? What made it feel that way?
2. Is there anything that makes learning in this class difficult for you?
3. What is one thing you enjoy about this class, and why?
4. What do you think the teacher could do to help you learn better?
5. What kinds of activities do you find the most engaging or interesting?
6. Do you feel like you can ask for help when you need it? Why or why not?
7. What is most fair about this class? What is most unfair? Why?

Possible Survey Questions

Scaled Questions (1–5 or Agree/Disagree):

1. I feel like I understand the expectations in this class.

2. I feel comfortable asking for help when I don't understand something.

3. I feel like my teacher cares about my learning.

4. I enjoy the activities we do in this class.

5. I feel like my classmates respect my ideas during discussions or group work.

Open-Ended Survey Questions

1. What's one thing you would like to do more often in this class?

2. If you could change one thing about the way we learn in this class, what would it be?

3. What helps you learn best?

4. Is there anything you'd like your teacher to know about you or how you learn?

After collecting the data, teams can organize responses by themes, identify commonalities, and note outliers to guide actionable steps. Then, to ensure that the feedback translates into meaningful classroom improvements, teams can analyze and collaboratively discuss their findings with representative quotes or visuals to prioritize high-impact, feasible changes. With thoughtful planning and execution, this approach not only strengthens teacher-student relationships but also drives a culture of continuous improvement.

ASK A BOT

The suggested questions in Figure 5.5 are meant to spark ideas for you, but we recognize that they may not address the common challenge you are investigating. As well, they may not be developmentally appropriate for your learners. If so, you can write a prompt for the chatbot that includes your common challenge and the major curricular and instructional actions you took during the investigation cycle. Then include information about the age or grade level of the students and request suggested interview and survey questions. As always, keep the human in the loop: Use your team's expertise to revise and refine questions that get at the information you are seeking. Use the following prompt as an example:

> Our team has the following common challenge: **[INSERT COMMON CHALLENGE]**. We have implemented the following strategies to address our challenge: **[INSERT STRATEGIES]**. What questions could we ask our students who are in **[IDENTIFY GRADE]**? We want to gain their perspective about our efforts and recommendations.

QUICK START

	I can start this tomorrow	I can begin this month	I need to discuss this with others	Resources needed
Design questions you can use with focal students. Consult other resources you have for suggested questions.				
Use interview techniques with students that foster a psychologically safe and supportive climate.				
Identify who will gather information from focal students.				
Consider your collective responsibility and the possibility of flexible grouping across teachers to meet the needs of students.				

Available for download at https://companion.corwin.com/courses/PLC

RETURNING TO THE COMMON CHALLENGE AFTER ANALYZING DATA

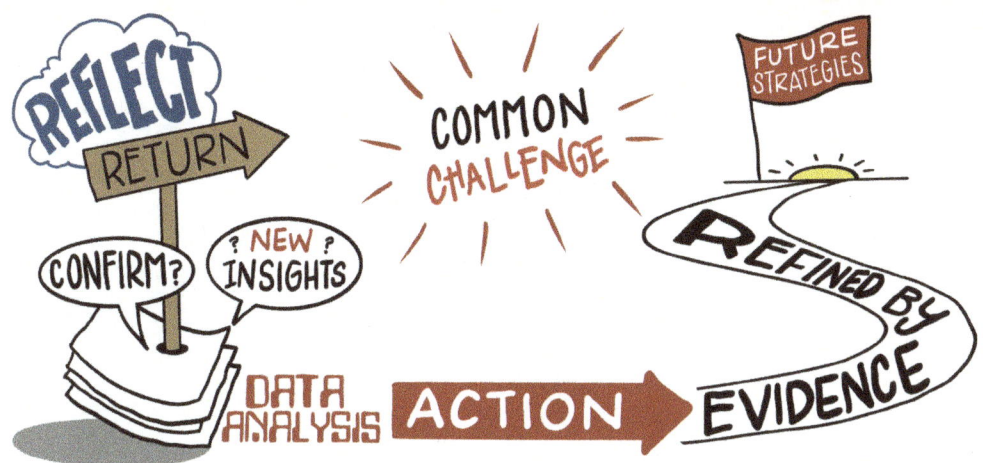

As we have discussed, it's important for teams to build in intentional pauses to *notice* and *reflect* on their emergent understanding throughout the process. Then, after analyzing the outcomes data, teams should return to the common challenge to reflect again on their progress and make decisions about next steps. By engaging the modes of *empathize* and *inquire* and/or prototyping and trying various safe-to-fail actions and interventions, teams will further evolve their understanding of the challenge.

After analyzing the data, teams should begin their reflection by revisiting the original challenge statement and evaluating it in light of the information that has been collected. Teams can ask, "Does the data confirm our initial understanding of the problem, or has our perspective shifted?" This reflection allows educators to assess whether their strategies are addressing the challenge effectively or if adjustments are required to achieve the desired outcomes. By anchoring discussions in the common challenge, teams maintain focus on their shared goals and create a clear pathway for refining their approach based on evidence.

This step also prompts teams to transition from analysis to action by leveraging the insights they have gained from the data to inform their future strategies. Reflection should include identifying both successes and areas where improvement is needed, asking questions like, "What worked well, and why?" and "What barriers still exist?" From there, teams can brainstorm actionable steps to address gaps, refine interventions, or explore alternative methods. Revisiting the common challenge in this way fosters a sense of collective efficacy while ensuring that next steps are directly tied to achieving meaningful, measurable progress. This process not only strengthens the team's focus but also builds momentum toward sustained improvement and positive outcomes for students.

The common challenge debriefing protocol draws upon several Liberatory Design modes: *see the system, define, inquire, notice and reflect,* and *imagine*. The intention is to prevent a postmortem discussion that leaves teams feeling they are at the end of something—without appreciating that the inquiry provides insight into a new beginning. The investigation cycles are rarely "one and done." As Senge noted in *Schools That Learn*, "The key to success isn't just thinking about what we are doing but doing something about what we are thinking."[97]

POST-INVESTIGATION COMMON CHALLENGE PROTOCOL WITH LIBERATORY DESIGN MODES

The common challenge has organized the team and focused their efforts. Teams should periodically review their progress and success, which can fuel collective efficacy and allow teams to make revisions intended to increase their impact.

Purpose: To collaboratively reflect on the investigation's outcomes, evaluate progress toward addressing the common challenge, and make informed decisions about next steps.

Imagine

STEP 1: Reflect on Outcomes and Revisit the Challenge (20 minutes)

Review Data and Insights (5 minutes)

- **Data Presentation**: Share outcomes data (quantitative and qualitative), highlighting patterns and significant findings.
- **Guiding Questions**:
  - What do the data reveal about the impact of our intervention for students most impacted by the challenge we addressed?
  - What unexpected results or insights emerged?

Reconnect With the Common Challenge (5 minutes)

- Revisit the original challenge statement.
- Discuss:
  - How do the data affirm or challenge our initial understanding of the issue?
  - Have new dimensions of the challenge emerged based on what we learned?
  - What implications does this have for how we move forward?

Collaborative Reflection (10 minutes)

- **Identify Successes and Gaps**:
  - What aspects of the investigation were successful, and why?
  - Where did we fall short, and what barriers remain?
- **Guiding Questions**:
  - Which student needs are still unmet?
  - How might we refine the challenge to reflect current understanding?
- **Action**: Revise the common challenge statement, if necessary, to align with new insights.

STEP 2: Plan for Next Steps (25 minutes)

Prioritize Needs and Opportunities (10 minutes)

- **Guiding Questions**:
  - Based on what we've learned, what should our next steps focus on?
  - Are there specific student groups or needs that require more attention?
- **Action**: Develop a prioritized list of focus areas for further action or investigation.

Design Adjustments and Extensions (10 minutes)

- **Modifications:** Brainstorm modifications to the intervention or plan new actions to address unmet needs.
- **Safe-to-Fail Actions**: Identify small, manageable steps to try and test revised approaches.
- **Guiding Questions**:
  - What changes can we implement to improve outcomes?
  - How will we measure success in the next iteration?
- Document agreed-upon next steps and assign roles to team members.

Reflection and Accountability (5 minutes)

- **Plus/Delta Feedback:**
  - What worked well in our intervention and data analysis process?
  - What do we want to appreciate about the ways we collaborated together?
  - What tensions or power dynamics impacted our work that are important to name and address as we continue our collaboration?
  - What could we do differently in future cycles?
- Schedule the next check-in to review progress and data.

STEP 3: Commit to Shared Responsibility (5 minutes)

- Reaffirm the team's commitment to the revised challenge and next steps.
- Identify support needed (e.g., professional development, additional resources).
- Close with a collective reflection on how this process strengthens collaboration and impacts student success.

Quality Checklist for Revisiting the Common Challenge

- ☐ Data are shared and analyzed in ways that honor the efforts put into the work.
- ☐ Teams address the realities represented in the data.
- ☐ Teams celebrate their success and identify next steps to foster students' learning.
- ☐ Teams reflect on their collaborative skills and identify learning opportunities for the team.

Video 5.5
A team works through the Post-Investigation Common Challenge Protocol
qrs.ly/hqghocq

CASE IN POINT: TOO QUICK TO ACT?

The Pine Tree Elementary PLC+ team gathered around a shared table, each teacher holding data reports and notes. The data visualizer showed that some students made a lot of progress and achieved well while others achieved well but did not progress in the lesson. Very few made progress but did not achieve a high level of success, and several did not benefit much from the experience (see Figure 5.6).

Lisa Simon, the kindergarten lead, opened the discussion. "Looking at our progress, I see that many of our students improved their ability to count forward and backward, but some are still struggling with one-to-one correspondence, especially during independent activities. I wonder if we need to revisit how we scaffold that skill."

Jorge Rojas, the first-grade teacher, nodded. "It's similar in my class. Most students are grasping the concept of grouping numbers, but there's a subset who aren't progressing with composing and decomposing numbers. I tried manipulatives, visual models, and even small-group interventions, but for these students, it's just not clicking yet."

Amy Chang, the intervention specialist, chimed in. "Did you notice if the struggling students are the same ones who struggled in kindergarten? We might need to look at their learning profiles and think about whether there's a foundational gap we're not addressing. Maybe it's not just the strategy, but also the frequency of practice or how we monitor their progress."

Figure 5.6 • Data Visualized

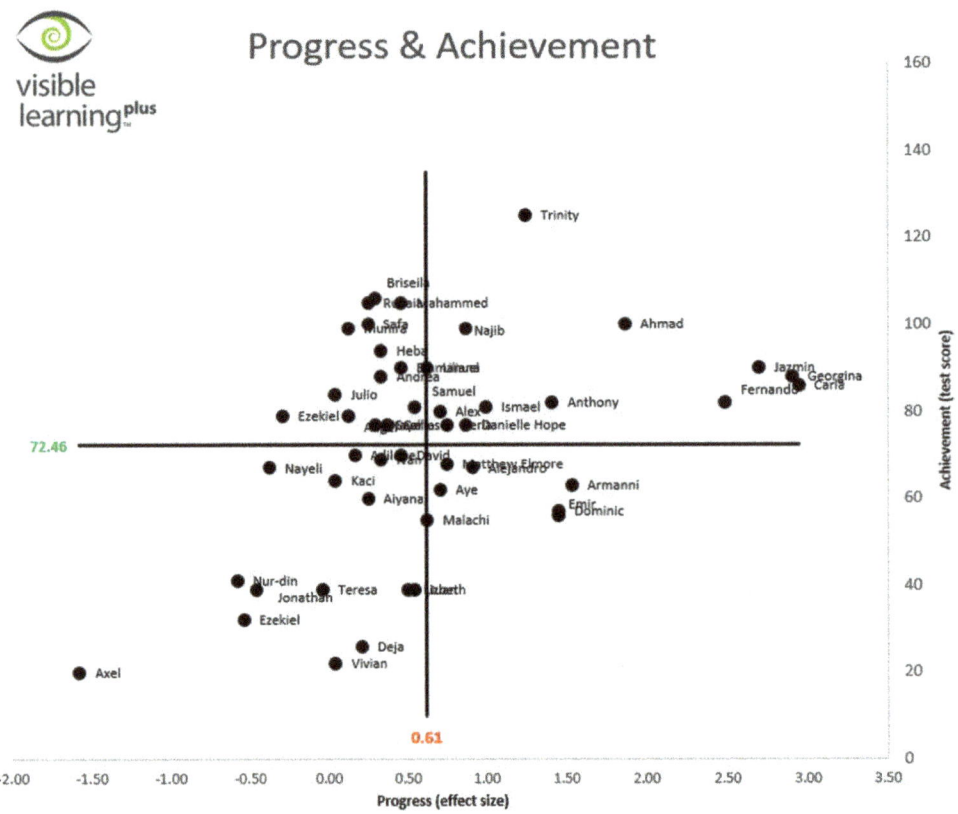

Retrieved from www.visiblelearning.com.

First-grade teacher Kimmy Watson said, "I like that idea of more hands-on activities, Jorge. And maybe we should design more take-home activities that families can do."

"I agree with all of you that there might be some good ideas to explore," Ms. Simon remarked. "But I feel like there's something more going on here. I think it's important to slow down in our analysis before making decisions. We need a more targeted plan, but we also need to make sure we're getting a complete picture and not just looking at test scores."

What's Your Advice?

- The team had collected other data, including measuring progress and achievement, and identifying focal students. However, they weren't using it. What are the risks they run in overlooking other data?

- The intervention specialist may have been onto something in suggesting they look at previous data. What other patterns and trends should they look for?

- Interviews with focal students might be enlightening. Suggest interview questions they could ask kindergarten and first-grade students to gain more information and insight.

Video 5.6
An activator reflects on the case in point
qrs.ly/77gi5ya

NOTES

CROSSCUTTING VALUES CHECK

How do teams discuss progress and achievement, noting the impact that they have had on students' learning? How has the common challenge sparked new ideas? Consider these reflective questions to spark discussion with colleagues.

Equity and Fairness

- In what ways do we partner with our focal students to learn about them and from them? How do we use this to leverage student learning?
- What did we learn about who is impacted by this common challenge and how they are experiencing it?
- What barriers have we identified, and what is our plan to remove or reduce them?

High Expectations

- What do we need to keep in mind when maintaining high expectations for all students?
- How do we evidence our high expectations for ourselves as individuals and as a learning community?
- How do measures of progress, along with measures of achievement, help us understand our expectations?

Individual and Collective Efficacy

- What reflections do we have about our collaboration?
- What did we experience as liberatory in our collaboration? What did not feel liberatory in our collaboration?
- What has our collaboration taught us about ourselves as individuals?

Activators

- In what ways has each of us been an activator during our investigation cycle?
- What can we celebrate as a team?
- How is what we learned in this investigation cycle informing new common challenges?

SELF-ASSESSMENT

Who Benefitted and Who Did Not?

This question requires a critical look at who did and did not make the expected learning gains as a result of our instruction. Because learning intentions, success criteria, and learning progressions provide the definition of "benefit," we must carefully consider what they've defined. To answer this question, teams must acknowledge and act upon any evidence that points to learners who did not benefit from their instruction. This also means identifying any commonalities among these learners. For example, are the learning experiences provided to those underperforming learners of the same quality as those provided to high-performing learners? Challenging an understanding of who is and isn't benefitting allows the team to professionally learn while also evolving its collaboration and implementation of instruction to the point of reaching all learners—not by chance, but by design.

Rapid Assessment:

We intentionally seek to identify patterns that suggest barriers to learning, monitor progress and achievement for all students, and modify instruction using strategies that include tiered systems, new approaches to instruction, and heightening collective efficacy.

1	2	3	4	5
Not Begun or Not Initiated	Very Limited Evidence of Capacity	Some Evidence of Capacity	Evidence of Capacity and Limited Evidence of Effective Implementation	Evidence of Capacity and Demonstrated Effective Implementation

Queries for Conducting a Detailed Assessment:

	Who Benefitted and Who Did Not?	Not Begun or Not Initiated	Very Limited Evidence of Capacity	Some Evidence of Capacity	Evidence of Capacity and Limited Evidence of Effective Implementation	Evidence of Capacity and Demonstrated Effective Implementation
5.1	We regularly identify, with evidence, patterns that may suggest underlying issues or barriers to learning.	1	2	3	4	5
5.2	We implement tiered systems of support based on individual student needs.	1	2	3	4	5
5.3	We modify instruction to address barriers to learning.	1	2	3	4	5
5.4	We regularly learn—as a team—new methods, strategies, or approaches.	1	2	3	4	5
5.5	Our work as a team reflects our collective efficacy.	1	2	3	4	5

Available for download at **https://companion.corwin.com/courses/PLC**

NOTICE AND REFLECT

 ### ESSENTIAL QUESTION

How can we see and remove barriers to learning?

THINK ABOUT

- Are we examining evidence of progress, not just mastery?
- Are we able to see the system that influences these results?
- Do we involve stakeholders in developing solutions?

START – STOP – KEEP

Based on what you learned in this module, answer the questions below.

Start: What practice(s) would you like to start doing?

Stop: What practice(s) would you like to stop doing?

Keep: What practice(s) would you like to keep doing?

NOTES

6 PLC+ PLANNING, PROGRESS MONITORING, AND SUCCESS TOOLS

As we have shown, the five PLC+ guiding questions are an important aspect of an effective PLC and the teams that meet to engage in the process. These questions are supported by protocols that allow teams to efficiently complete their tasks and remain focused on their work. The protocols also help teams continue to build and maintain their collaborative maturity: their current maximum capability to collaborate through effective communication, shared understandings, and the adjustment of tasks and behaviors to produce high-quality outcomes.[98]

Teams should regularly assess their efforts and engage in intentional actions that foster each of the following aspects of collaboration and collective efficacy:

- Effective communication on a team is vital if members are going to feel heard and develop a sense of belonging to the group. Belonging is more than a feeling of inclusion or being seen. "Belonging means that your well-being is considered" and "entails having a meaningful voice and the opportunity to participate in the design of social and cultural structures."[99] Belonging is a prerequisite to engagement; when we feel that we belong, we are much more likely to contribute to our groups.

- Shared understandings are valuable as they allow teams to move faster because language and vocabulary are clear. Shared understandings come in many forms, including common challenges that provide a focus for teams' time together as well as decision-making processes that allow teams to commit to a course of action.

- Adjusting tasks and behaviors allows teams—and the individuals on those teams—to increase their impact as they recognize that there may be more effective and efficient ways to ensure students' learning.

The planning, progress monitoring, and success tools included in this module are designed to foster collaborative maturity and increase the value proposition of the PLC+ process. When educators see value in their time together, realizing that they are having an impact on each other and on their students, then they recognize that the time spent with their peers is a wise investment.

Essential Question

HOW DO WE KNOW THE LEVEL OF SUCCESS OF OUR TEAM, AND HOW CAN WE EXTEND OUR REACH AND IMPACT?

Video 6.1
Nancy overviews planning, progress monitoring, and success tools
qrs.ly/wnghocr

NOTES

TWO TRUTHS AND A LIE

***Two of these statements are true; one is false.
Can you spot the lie?***

1. A goal of PLCs is that members develop collective responsibility for students' learning.
2. Common formative assessments are an important part of the PLC process.
3. School leaders can support PLCs by providing time and respect for teachers to learn from each other.

Collective responsibility was an original goal for professional learning communities as teacher isolation was far too common in the 1950s and 1960s. The realization was that groups of teachers had the potential to meet more students' needs than every teacher trying to meet the needs of all students. The key elements of collective responsibility include the following:[100]

- All staff members share a commitment to the success of each student.
- Educators do not allow any single teacher to fail in their attempt to ensure the success of any one student.
- Students benefit from the wisdom and expertise of all teachers, rather than just of the teachers to whom they are assigned.
- Teachers willingly share what is working in their classrooms with their colleagues.
- Teachers with less experience realize that other teachers are invested in their success and the success of all students.

Number 2 is the lie. Teams need evidence for their discussions, but there are many forms of evidence. Restricting conversations to a common formative assessment reduces the potential of team members to explore student learning across a variety of dimensions. In addition, teams can spend way too much time developing a common assessment, which is time that is taken away from moving learning forward. Again, analyzing and interpreting evidence is important, but teachers are awash with data, and they need time to think about those data rather than always spending time making new assessments.

Thus, statement 3 is also true. It's important for leaders to support teacher teams and provide them with time, respect, and support for the implementation of the PLC+ process. Without leadership support, teacher teams and the entire PLC+ process will be compromised.[101] Leaders establish, maintain, and repair the climate and culture of the school, and that includes the systems of support for teachers to collaborate and learn from one another.[102]

PLANNING FOR SUCCESS: THE PLUS IS YOU

Long before we are educators, we are humans. And as humans we bring to every situation our experiences, personalities, perspectives, and concerns. We don't leave those at the classroom door because we are now at school. As such, all our colleagues bring their own unique brew. True collaboration requires not only that we are self-reflective about how our perspectives are shaded by our experiences, but also that we are willing to help others in being reflective as a team.

A sense of belonging is fundamental to the success of any team, including PLCs. When team members feel valued, included, and connected, they are more likely to contribute authentically and collaborate effectively. Belonging fosters trust, mutual respect, and a shared commitment to team goals, creating a positive and productive environment.

Belonging also ensures that team members feel their voices matter, which is essential for meaningful dialogue and decision-making. When educators feel secure and appreciated, they are more willing to share their perspectives, take risks, and engage in critical reflection. This openness enables the team to leverage diverse ideas, resulting in innovative solutions and improved outcomes for students. A culture of belonging also builds collective efficacy—the belief that the team can achieve more together than individually—a key driver of student achievement.

Conversely, a lack of belonging undermines team effectiveness in significant ways. When members feel excluded, undervalued, or disconnected, they may disengage or withhold contributions, limiting the team's potential. Fear of judgment or rejection can stifle creativity and honest feedback, preventing the team from addressing challenges effectively. Moreover, a lack of belonging erodes trust and collaboration, leading to silos and conflict rather than unity and purpose.

To cultivate belonging, teams must prioritize inclusivity, celebrate diverse perspectives, and establish norms that promote equity and respect. When every member feels seen, heard, and valued, the team becomes a powerful force for growth and improvement, benefiting both educators and students alike.

We have been inspired by the work of Eric Carter's model of belonging.[103] While his original work focused on sense of belonging for people with intellectual disabilities, we have seen the universality in these eleven dimensions of belonging. For each of the factors identified, we provide a definition and a reflection question. Our experience suggests that each of them plays a role in whether or not a team member believes that they belong.

Figure 6.1 • Dimensions of Belonging on a Team

- **PRESENT.** This factor relates to attendance: Who is actually present at team meetings? Some people miss a lot of meetings because they do not feel that they belong.

    Reflection: *Do we ensure that all members are present for discussions whenever possible?*

- **INVITED.** The ways in which people are invited signals their value and fosters a sense of belonging. We have all experienced an obligatory invitation, knowing full well that we really didn't belong.

    Reflection: *Do we actively extend invitations to all appropriate team members?*

- **WELCOMED.** The way we are greeted each time we meet our team members signals their importance and fosters belonging.

    Reflection: *Are we extending a warm welcome to our colleagues each time we gather as a team?*

- **KNOWN.** Do we know our colleagues—really know them? Or do we only know others on the surface level? When people have a strong sense of belonging, they want to share who they are and what they care about with others.

    Reflection: *Do we know our colleagues personally and for the strengths they possess?*

- **ACCEPTED.** We all have strengths and personalities, but we don't always feel accepted for who we are. Accepted means that we're recognized as individuals and recognized as a member of the group.

    Reflection: *Are we receiving our colleagues unconditionally and graciously?*

- **INVOLVED.** As we noted in the definition of belonging, members of groups want to know that their contributions are valued, which requires that we are involved in the tasks and workflow of the group.

    Reflection: *Are team members actively engaged with, and alongside, colleagues in shared learning and common goals?*

(Continued)

(Continued)

- **SUPPORTED.** We've noted this several times, but each of us has needs, personalities, and differences. When we feel supported—that there is recognition of our uniqueness—we are more likely to participate and to contribute in ways that support the group.

  Reflection: *Do we provide the assistance our colleagues need to participate fully and meaningfully?*

- **HEARD.** Actively listening to others telegraphs a message that they are valued and that they have ideas worth considering. When we feel heard, our satisfaction with the experience increases, even if the decision is not consistent with our initial recommendations. Feeling heard tells us that our feelings, beliefs, and thoughts are meaningful.

- **Reflection:** *Are we seeking out our colleagues' perspectives on issues that matter?*

- **BEFRIENDED.** Being friendly with others signals that they belong. We are not suggesting that all team members need to develop strong bonds that extend beyond the school day; rather, we are noting that there is a social aspect to the ways in which groups work.

- **Reflection:** *Are we creating opportunities for socialization between our colleagues?*

- **NEEDED.** When others rely on us, we know that our contributions are valued, and we deepen our commitment to the team. The opposite is also true. If the team can accomplish the work without some of the members, then those who are not needed feel it and recognize that they do not belong.

- **Reflection:** *Are we recognizing and receiving our colleagues' talents, gifts, and contributions?*

- **LOVED.** There are many types of love, and some people are cynical about loving their colleagues. The Greeks noted that there are many different types of love, including romantic love and love for your family. When it comes to belonging on a team, we're talking about *agape*: the selfless, unconditional love that conveys compassion and empathy.

- **Reflection:** *Do we love our colleagues unconditionally, demonstrating empathy and compassion for them as individuals?*

Video 6.2
Adults discuss belonging on a team
qrs.ly/9lghoct

Source: Lassiter, C., Fisher, D., Faddis, T., & Frey, N. (2024).

NOTES

MONITORING FOR SUCCESS: THE PLUS IS US

Engaging in open and reflective discussions, including self-reflection, is a cornerstone of effective teams.[104] Such practices are vital for fostering a collaborative culture where educators critically examine their teaching, analyze student outcomes, and develop strategies to enhance learning. This process aligns with the core purpose of professional learning communities: ensuring high levels of learning for all students through collective responsibility and expertise.

Open dialogue within the team creates a space for sharing diverse perspectives, enabling deeper insights into instructional practices and student needs. When educators feel safe to express their thoughts, challenge assumptions, and question existing methods, the team can collaboratively evaluate what works and what doesn't. Reflective discussions, particularly those that integrate self-reflection, allow team members to identify their individual areas for growth while considering how their practices contribute to the collective goals. This dual reflection—on the self and on the team—ensures a more comprehensive approach to professional growth.

Self-reflection enhances the depth of these conversations by encouraging educators to honestly assess their strengths, challenges, and the impact of their actions on student learning. When educators come prepared with personal insights, the team benefits from more focused and meaningful discussions. This personal accountability promotes continuous improvement, as individuals commit to refining their practices in alignment with shared goals.

Moreover, reflective discussions that integrate self-reflection build trust and collective efficacy within PLCs. When educators demonstrate vulnerability by sharing their reflections and seeking feedback, they strengthen relationships and foster a culture of mutual support. This collaborative spirit reinforces high expectations for both educators and students, creating a dynamic environment for sustained improvement.

Having said that, it can be difficult to get a reflective discussion going. The National Equity Project has a series of discussion starters that can spark valuable discussion (Figure 6.2). We advise incorporating at least one into each meeting to build the habit of engaging in self-reflection and team reflection. Ultimately, teams that embrace open dialogue and self-reflection create a powerful synergy, enabling them to respond effectively to challenges and drive transformative change in their classrooms and schools.

Figure 6.2 • Prompts to Support and Deepen Liberatory Collaboration

INDIVIDUAL

- What have I learned about myself and my leadership? How have I grown? How would I like to grow?
- What fears and insecurities did I overcome or witness others overcome?
- What fears and insecurities held me back? What are my reflections about that?

TEAM DYNAMICS

- What reflections do we have about our collaboration?
- What is important for us to keep in mind about our work together moving forward?
- What did we experience as liberatory in our collaboration? What did not feel liberatory about our collaboration?
- What tensions surfaced in our work?
- How are power dynamics impacting our work?
- What is something important we learned about a team member?

CELEBRATIONS

- What can we celebrate?
- Who and what do we appreciate about our work?
- What stances, mindsets, skills, actions, and conditions supported our progress and/or learning?
- What fears and insecurities did we witness others overcome?

SEE THE SYSTEM

- What did we learn about our specific inquiry questions?
- What did we learn about our equity challenge and the factors that may be contributing to this challenge?
- What did we learn about who is impacted by this equity challenge and how they are experiencing it?
- What implications does all this have for our next leadership steps?
- What are we still wondering about? What new questions have emerged?

Source: Prompts to Support and Deepen Liberatory Collaboration, National Equity Project.

BUILDING FOR SUCCESS WITH THE PLC+ READINESS ASSESSMENT TOOL

Informed by Shirley Hord's research-defined indicators for PLC success, the PLC+ Readiness Assessment Tool can serve as a helpful guide for planning and implementation. There are six domains:

- Firm foundations for collaborative teams
- Supportive relationships and collegial processes
- Shared vision and values
- Intentional collective learning
- Peers supporting peers
- Shared and supportive leadership

These six domains, which we discuss in more detail shortly, largely focus on ensuring that PLC+ teams consider, plan, and implement the conditions needed to successfully support their initiative. As teams work together, they can use the tool to monitor and track progress and to make informed adjustments to the PLC+ initiative, thus iteratively increasing the promise of predictable results.

DOMAIN 1: PLC+ FIRM FOUNDATION

For each **Firm Foundation** indicator, explore the assessment questions with your team. Develop consensus, based on evidence available and discussion, around your current state for each indicator. Then assign the corresponding criteria based on the five-point scale.

NEEDS ASSESSMENT SCALE

Use this form to explore your readiness for a PLC+ initiative. Consider each of the five indicators and your school's or district's past efforts. Then, select a point on the scale that represents your current capacity, experience, or readiness to fulfill what each indicator describes.

	Our planned PLC+ initiative will be supported by:	Nothing in Place	Not a Current Strength	Some Demonstrated Capacity	Demonstrated Capacity in Place	Exemplary Capacity in Place
1.1	Dedicated PLC+ teams who engage the right people.	1	2	3	4	5
1.2	Dedicated time that is provided each week, at a minimum, for meetings that solely focus on the PLC+ initiative.	1	2	3	4	5
1.3	Access to necessary resources, such as shared technology, collaboration tools, and so on, that make the PLC+ work efficient and effective.	1	2	3	4	5
1.4	Access to the appropriate data, in usable formats, that support the PLC+ initiative's focus.	1	2	3	4	5
1.5	Access to disaggregated data in pursuit of understanding strengths and needs based on student performance over time.	1	2	3	4	5

Available for download at https://companion.corwin.com/courses/PLC

PLC+ IN PROGRESS ASSESSMENT SCALE

Use this form to explore your PLC+ initiative's progress and current levels of success. Consider each of the five indicators and your current efforts. Then, select a point on the scale that represents your current capacity, experience, or operation in fulfilling what each indicator describes.

	Our PLC+ initiative is supported by:	Not Begun	Partial	Emergent	Established	Exemplary
1.1	Dedicated PLC+ teams who engage the right people.	1	2	3	4	5
1.2	Dedicated time that is provided each week, at a minimum, for meetings that solely focus on the PLC+ initiative.	1	2	3	4	5
1.3	Access to necessary resources, such as shared technology, collaboration tools, and so on, that make the PLC+ work efficient and effective.	1	2	3	4	5
1.4	Access to appropriate data, in usable formats, that support the PLC+ initiative's focus.	1	2	3	4	5
1.5	Access to disaggregated data in pursuit of understanding strengths and needs based on student performance over time.	1	2	3	4	5

Available for download at https://companion.corwin.com/courses/PLC

The following questions will guide your team's assessment of the PLC+ **Firm Foundation** domain.

	Our PLC+ initiative is:	Assessment Considerations
1.1	Dedicated PLC+ teams who engage the right people.	• Who is invited and who is excluded from the PLC+? • Who have we not included that is necessary for a high-performing PLC+ initiative? • To what degree are PLC+ members engaged? How do we plan to keep them engaged?
1.2	Dedicated time that is provided each week, at a minimum, for meetings that solely focus on the PLC+ initiative.	• Is there dedicated time set aside each day, or each week, for the PLC+ to meet? • Is the time allotted sufficient to the point where we agree that the PLC+ initiative is moving forward with success? • Do other priorities often preclude some PLC+ members from being present consistently?
1.3	Access to necessary resources, such as shared technology, collaboration tools, and so on, that make the PLC+ work efficient and effective.	• Are the resources we need to function as a PLC+ present? • To what extent do provided resources that should be used go unused or underutilized? • What resources are currently not available, yet needed by the PLC+?
1.4	Access to appropriate data, in usable formats, that support the PLC+ initiative's focus.	• What data are available to PLC+ members? What data remain unavailable or inaccessible? • Do PLC+ members have to lobby for permissions to access data that are critical to the PLC+ initiative? • Are the available data in a format that is easy to understand and universally accessible to all PLC+ members?
1.5	Access to disaggregated data in pursuit of understanding strengths and needs based on student performance over time.	• Has leadership provided PLC+ members with access to data experts who can support the community's data needs and requests? • Are requests for critical data related to the PLC+ initiative given priority? • Do data consultations regularly focus on—and do PLC+ discussions revolve around—student strengths and needs?

 Available for download at **https://companion.corwin.com/courses/PLC**

DOMAIN 2: SUPPORTIVE RELATIONSHIPS AND COLLEGIAL PROCESSES

For each indicator, explore the assessment questions with your team. Develop consensus, based on evidence available and discussion, around your current state for each **Supportive Relationships and Collegial Processes** indicator. Then assign the corresponding criteria, based on the five-point scale.

NOTES

NEEDS ASSESSMENT

Use this form to explore your readiness for a PLC+ initiative. Consider each of the five indicators and your school's or district's past efforts. Then, select a point on the scale that represents your current capacity, experience, or readiness to fulfill what each indicator describes.

	Our planned PLC+ initiative will involve:	Nothing in Place	Not a Current Strength	Some Demonstrated Capacity	Demonstrated Capacity in Place	Exemplary Capacity in Place
2.1	PLC+ members who respect one another.	1	2	3	4	5
2.2	Conversation styles and interactions that reflect regard for one another.	1	2	3	4	5
2.3	Confronting conflict, when necessary, in supportive and effective ways.	1	2	3	4	5
2.4	A commitment to, and practice of, all PLC+ members having a voice in the PLC+.	1	2	3	4	5
2.5	A demonstrated level of trust among PLC+ members.	1	2	3	4	5

online resources: Available for download at **https://companion.corwin.com/courses/PLC**

PLC+ IN PROGRESS ASSESSMENT

Use this form to explore your PLC+ initiative's progress and current levels of success. Consider each of the five indicators and your current efforts. Then, select a point on the scale that represents your current capacity, experience, or operation in fulfilling what each indicator describes.

	Our PLC+ initiative involves:	Not Begun	Partial	Emergent	Established	Exemplary
2.1	PLC+ members who respect one another.	1	2	3	4	5
2.2	Conversation styles and interactions that reflect regard for one another.	1	2	3	4	5
2.3	Confronting conflict, when necessary, in supportive and effective ways.	1	2	3	4	5
2.4	A commitment to, and practice of, all PLC+ members having a voice in the PLC+.	1	2	3	4	5
2.5	A demonstrated level of trust among PLC+ members.	1	2	3	4	5

Available for download at **https://companion.corwin.com/courses/PLC**

The following questions will guide your team's assessment of the PLC+ **Supportive Relationships and Collegial Processes** domain.

	Our PLC+ initiative involves:	Assessment Considerations
2.1	PLC+ members who respect one another.	• What tangible evidence do we have of mutual respect among PLC+ members? • When observing PLC+ member interactions, are we able to point to behaviors to demonstrate respect across the team? • Do opportunities remain to foster, support, or increase respect among PLC+ members?
2.2	Conversation styles and interactions that reflect regard for one another.	• When observing PLC+ member interactions, are we able to point to behaviors to demonstrate regard for one another across the team? • How would we describe the conversation styles of PLC+ members? • How would we describe the interactions among PLC+ members?
2.3	Confronting conflict, when necessary, in supportive and effective ways.	• When conflict arises, are we open to addressing it directly? • Is the discussion of conflict a shared discussion, or largely the voices of a few PLC+ members? • Is the resolution of conflict viewed as fair and just by PLC+ members?
2.4	A commitment to, and practice of, all PLC+ members having a voice in the PLC+.	• Are the voices of all PLC+ members contributed in each meeting? • Do PLC+ members take action when they observe limited participation from their peers? • Does each PLC+ member feel and believe their voice is valued in the community?
2.5	A demonstrated level of trust among PLC+ members.	• What tangible, measurable evidence do we have that demonstrates trust among PLC+ members? • In what ways do PLC+ members trust one another? • Are there observed limits to the boundaries of trust? Consider content- and interaction-related elements.

 Available for download at **https://companion.corwin.com/courses/PLC**

DOMAIN 3: SHARED VISION AND VALUES

For each indicator, explore the assessment questions with your team. Develop consensus, based on evidence available and discussion, around your current state for each **Shared Vision and Values** indicator. Then assign the corresponding criteria, based on the five-point scale.

NOTES

NEEDS ASSESSMENT

Use this form to explore your readiness for a PLC+ initiative. Consider each of the five indicators and your school's or district's past efforts. Then, select a point on the scale that represents your current capacity, experience, or readiness to fulfill what each indicator describes.

	Our planned PLC+ initiative will be:	Nothing in Place	Not a Current Strength	Some Demonstrated Capacity	Demonstrated Capacity in Place	Exemplary Capacity in Place
3.1	Grounded in a shared vision for our school.	1	2	3	4	5
3.2	Benefitting from shared values reached through PLC+ consensus.	1	2	3	4	5
3.3	Pursuing new strategies and processes we have agreed upon.	1	2	3	4	5
3.4	Calibrated as to how our shared vision and values will be implemented.	1	2	3	4	5
3.5	Implemented with defined, observable, and measurable actions that are clearly aligned with our stated vision and values.	1	2	3	4	5

Available for download at **https://companion.corwin.com/courses/PLC**

PLC+ IN PROGRESS ASSESSMENT

Use this form to explore your PLC+ initiative's progress and current levels of success. Consider each of the five indicators and your current efforts. Then, select a point on the scale that represents your current capacity, experience, or operation in fulfilling what each indicator describes.

	Our PLC+ initiative is:	Not Begun	Partial	Emergent	Established	Exemplary
3.1	Grounded in a shared vision for our school.	1	2	3	4	5
3.2	Benefitting from shared values reached through PLC+ consensus.	1	2	3	4	5
3.3	Pursuing new strategies and processes we have agreed upon.	1	2	3	4	5
3.4	Calibrated as to how our shared vision and values will be implemented.	1	2	3	4	5
3.5	Implemented with defined, observable, and measurable actions that are clearly aligned with our stated vision and values.	1	2	3	4	5

Available for download at **https://companion.corwin.com/courses/PLC**

The following questions will guide your team's assessment of the PLC+ **Shared Vision and Values** domain.

Our PLC+ initiative is:		Assessment Considerations
3.1	Grounded in a shared vision for our school.	• How do we describe the shared vision for our school—and is it memorialized for ongoing reference? • Is the shared vision for our school something that is regularly consulted during PLC+ meetings? • In what ways does our PLC+ progress to date reflect the shared vision we have developed?
3.2	Benefitting from shared values reached through PLC+ consensus.	• How do we describe the shared values for our PLC+—and are those values memorialized for ongoing reference? • Are the shared values for our PLC+ regularly consulted during PLC+ meetings? • In what ways does our PLC+ progress to date reflect the shared values that we have developed for our PLC+?
3.3	Pursuing new strategies and processes we have agreed upon.	• Has our PLC+ developed new strategies and/or processes? • To what extent have we pursued new strategies and/or processes? • How are we monitoring the new strategies and/or processes to determine their effectiveness and pursue continuous improvement?
3.4	Calibrated as to how our shared vision and values will be implemented.	• What evidence do we have to suggest the PLC+ members' understanding of vision and values is truly understood and shared in similar ways? • Is there agreement among the PLC+ members as to how the vision and values will be or currently are implemented? • What opportunities remain that would result in better calibration and shared efforts, specific to the vision and values of the PLC+ initiative?
3.5	Implemented with defined, observable, and measurable actions that are clearly aligned with our stated vision and values.	• Are the shared decisions we have made to date consistent with our stated vision and values? • Are we able to point to actions we have taken and things we have implemented that directly align, and are responsive to, our stated vision and values? • Do we invest in determining the impact of the PLC+ implemented work specific to its alignment with, and impact on, our stated vision and values?

 Available for download at **https://companion.corwin.com/courses/PLC**

DOMAIN 4: INTENTIONAL COLLECTIVE LEARNING

For each indicator, explore the assessment questions with your team. Develop consensus, based on evidence available and discussion, around your current state for each **Intentional Collective Learning** indicator. Then assign the corresponding criteria, based on the five-point scale.

NOTES

NEEDS ASSESSMENT

Use this form to explore your readiness for a PLC+ initiative. Consider each of the five indicators and your school's or district's past efforts. Then, select a point on the scale that represents your current capacity, experience, or readiness to fulfill what each indicator describes.

	Our planned PLC+ initiative:	Nothing in Place	Not a Current Strength	Some Demonstrated Capacity	Demonstrated Capacity in Place	Exemplary Capacity in Place
4.1	Prioritizes continuous learning of the PLC+ members.	1	2	3	4	5
4.2	Determines what will be learned based on the PLC+ members' students' needs.	1	2	3	4	5
4.3	Prioritizes learning priorities based on the PLC+ members' students' needs.	1	2	3	4	5
4.4	Benefits from PLC+ member input as to the "how" of our intentional and continuous learning.	1	2	3	4	5
4.5	Features outcomes that are observable and measurable such that progress can be monitored and impact can be confirmed.	1	2	3	4	5

Available for download at **https://companion.corwin.com/courses/PLC**

PLC+ IN PROGRESS ASSESSMENT

Use this form to explore your PLC+ initiative's progress and current levels of success. Consider each of the five indicators and your current efforts. Then, select a point on the scale that represents your current capacity, experience, or operation in fulfilling what each indicator describes.

	Our PLC+ initiative:	Not Begun	Partial	Emergent	Established	Exemplary
4.1	Prioritizes continuous learning of the PLC+ members.	1	2	3	4	5
4.2	Determines what will be learned based on the PLC+ members' students' needs.	1	2	3	4	5
4.3	Prioritizes learning priorities based on the PLC+ members' students' needs.	1	2	3	4	5
4.4	Benefits from PLC+ member input as to the "how" of our intentional and continuous learning.	1	2	3	4	5
4.5	Features outcomes that are observable and measurable such that progress can be monitored and impact can be confirmed.	1	2	3	4	5

online resources Available for download at **https://companion.corwin.com/courses/PLC**

The following questions will guide your team's assessment of the PLC+ **Intentional Collective Learning** domain.

Our PLC+ initiative:		Assessment Considerations
4.1	Prioritizes continuous learning of the PLC+ members.	• What evidence do we have that continuous learning is acted upon as a key priority of the PLC+ initiative? • Has continuous learning been strategically planned and implemented as a key priority of the PLC+ initiative? • Have other competing priorities limited or lessened the amount of continuous, collective learning that has taken place?
4.2	Determines what will be learned based on the PLC+ members' students' needs.	• Are student strengths and needs regularly assessed and discussed in the PLC+? • To what extent do student strengths and needs influence the collective learning of PLC+ members? • Can we point to direct connections between (a) documented student strengths and needs and (b) continuous learning priorities established by PLC+ members?
4.3	Prioritizes learning priorities based on the PLC+ members' students' needs.	• Is there a direct relationship between the PLC+ members' learning priorities and reviewed student data? • In what ways do PLC+ learning priorities diverge from established student needs? • What evidence do we have that our learning priorities have been successfully addressed in the professional learning that has taken place to date?
4.4	Benefits from PLC+ member input as to the "how" of our intentional and continuous learning.	• Does our continuous learning reflect the input and needs of our PLC+? • Do PLC+ members have opportunities to inform, guide, and optimize the continuous learning efforts over time? • Does our continuous learning employ contemporary strategies that are geared toward efficient implementation as viewed by PLC+ member input?
4.5	Features outcomes that are observable and measurable such that progress can be monitored and impact can be confirmed.	• Have we defined observable and measurable outcomes for our continuous learning? • Do we seek opportunities to monitor and evaluate the implementation of our continuous learning, in support of continuous improvement? • What evidence do we have that our continuous learning decisions have resulted in a reasonable return on the investment?

online resources Available for download at **https://companion.corwin.com/courses/PLC**

DOMAIN 5: PEERS SUPPORTING PEERS

For each indicator, explore the assessment questions with your team. Develop consensus, based on evidence available and discussion, around your current state for each **Peers Supporting Peers** indicator. Then assign the corresponding criteria, based on the five-point scale.

NOTES

NEEDS ASSESSMENT

Use this form to explore your readiness for a PLC+ initiative. Consider each of the five indicators and your school's or district's past efforts. Then, select a point on the scale that represents your current capacity, experience, or readiness to fulfill what each indicator describes.

	Our planned PLC+ initiative depends upon:	Nothing in Place	Not a Current Strength	Some Demonstrated Capacity	Demonstrated Capacity in Place	Exemplary Capacity in Place
5.1	A balanced approach where PLC+ members host visits to their classrooms, while also making visits to peer classrooms.	1	2	3	4	5
5.2	PLC+ members observing one another's classrooms to understand and strengthen practice.	1	2	3	4	5
5.3	A commitment to sharing and receiving constructive feedback in the spirit of continuous improvement.	1	2	3	4	5
5.4	An observation process that includes observation, documentation, and collegial sharing of feedback.	1	2	3	4	5
5.5	A supportive climate where observation and feedback are sought, welcomed, and valued.	1	2	3	4	5

Available for download at **https://companion.corwin.com/courses/PLC**

PLC+ IN PROGRESS ASSESSMENT

Use this form to explore your PLC+ initiative's progress and current levels of success. Consider each of the five indicators and your current efforts. Then, select a point on the scale that represents your current capacity, experience, or operation in fulfilling what each indicator describes.

	Our PLC+ initiative depends upon:	Not Begun	Partial	Emergent	Established	Exemplary
5.1	A balanced approach where PLC+ members host visits to their classrooms, while also making visits to peer classrooms.	1	2	3	4	5
5.2	PLC+ members observing one another's classrooms to understand and strengthen practice.	1	2	3	4	5
5.3	A commitment to sharing and receiving constructive feedback in the spirit of continuous improvement.	1	2	3	4	5
5.4	An observation process that includes observation, documentation, and collegial sharing of feedback.	1	2	3	4	5
5.5	A supportive climate where observation and feedback are sought, welcomed, and valued.	1	2	3	4	5

Available for download at **https://companion.corwin.com/courses/PLC**

The following questions will guide your team's assessment of the PLC+ **Peers Supporting Peers** domain.

	Our PLC+ initiative depends upon:	Assessment Considerations
5.1	A balanced approach where PLC+ members host visits to their classrooms, while also making visits to peer classrooms.	• Is the expectation to both host classroom visits and make classroom visits well known throughout the PLC+? • Has each of the PLC+ members hosted a visit to their classroom? • Have all PLC+ members visited the classrooms of their peers?
5.2	PLC+ members observing one another's classrooms to understand and strengthen practice.	• Do PLC+ members understand and agree that the purpose of classroom visits is to understand and strengthen practice? • Has the PLC+ discussed classroom visits to assess the extent to which the process is helping the participants better understand, and then strengthen, practice? • In what ways can we continuously improve the classroom visit and learning process?
5.3	A commitment to sharing and receiving constructive feedback in the spirit of continuous improvement.	• Do PLC+ members understand and agree to the purposes of receiving constructive feedback? • How do PLC+ members describe the utility of the feedback they receive from their peers? • Can the PLC+ point to specific and measurable improvement made as a result of constructive feedback?
5.4	An observation process that includes observation, documentation, and collegial sharing of feedback.	• Does the PLC+ have an established observation process that includes observation, documentation, and collegial sharing of feedback? • Does the observation process allow teams to gather and share ideas? • Have the observations conducted to date fully aligned with the PLC+'s defined process?
5.5	A supportive climate where observation and feedback are sought, welcomed, and valued.	• How do PLC+ members describe the PLC+ climate specific to observation and feedback? • Are PLC+ members' descriptions consistent to the point of suggesting a shared view? • Do PLC+ members typically seek observation and feedback, or is it typically observed until required?

 Available for download at **https://companion.corwin.com/courses/PLC**

DOMAIN 6: SHARED AND SUPPORTIVE LEADERSHIP

For each indicator, explore the assessment questions with your team. Develop consensus, based on evidence available and discussion, around your current state for each **Shared and Supportive Leadership** indicator. Then assign the corresponding criteria, based on the five-point scale.

NOTES

NEEDS ASSESSMENT

Use this form to explore your readiness for a PLC+ initiative. Consider each of the five indicators and your school's or district's past efforts. Then, select a point on the scale that represents your current capacity, experience, or readiness to fulfill what each indicator describes.

	In our planned PLC+ initiative:	Nothing in Place	Not a Current Strength	Some Demonstrated Capacity	Demonstrated Capacity in Place	Exemplary Capacity in Place
6.1	The site or district leader(s) create opportunities for teachers to assume PLC+ leadership roles, resulting in distributed leadership.	1	2	3	4	5
6.2	The site or district leader(s) provide direct support to teachers who assume PLC+ leadership roles.	1	2	3	4	5
6.3	The site or district leader(s) share PLC+ decision-making with the PLC+ members, offering them voice and choice in the operation of their PLC+.	1	2	3	4	5
6.4	The shared and supportive leadership contributes to PLC+ members' feelings of efficacy within their schools.	1	2	3	4	5
6.5	The shared and supportive leadership contributes to measurably increased levels of trust between site or district leader(s) and PLC+ members.	1	2	3	4	5

Available for download at **https://companion.corwin.com/courses/PLC**

PLC+ IN PROGRESS ASSESSMENT

Use this form to explore your PLC+ initiative's progress and current levels of success. Consider each of the five indicators and your current efforts. Then, select a point on the scale that represents your current capacity, experience, or operation in fulfilling what each indicator describes.

	In our PLC+ initiative:	Not Begun	Partial	Emergent	Established	Exemplary
6.1	The site or district leader(s) create opportunities for teachers to assume PLC+ leadership roles, resulting in distributed leadership.	1	2	3	4	5
6.2	The site or district leader(s) provide direct support to teachers who assume PLC+ leadership roles.	1	2	3	4	5
6.3	The site or district leader(s) share PLC+ decision-making with the PLC+ members, offering them voice and choice in the operation of their PLC+.	1	2	3	4	5
6.4	The shared and supportive leadership contributes to PLC+ members' feelings of efficacy within their schools.	1	2	3	4	5
6.5	The shared and supportive leadership contributes to measurably increased levels of trust between site or district leader(s) and PLC+ members.	1	2	3	4	5

online resources — Available for download at **https://companion.corwin.com/courses/PLC**

The following questions will guide your team's assessment of the PLC+ **Shared and Supportive Leadership** domain.

In our PLC+ initiative effort:		Assessment Considerations
6.1	The site or district leader(s) create opportunities for teachers to assume PLC+ leadership roles, resulting in distributed leadership.	• Who are the leaders in the PLC+? • What leadership opportunities exist for members within the PLC+? • Have PLC+ members without significant leadership experience been tapped for PLC+ leadership roles?
6.2	The site or district leader(s) provide direct support to teachers who assume PLC+ leadership roles.	• How do teacher-leaders in the PLC+ describe the support they receive? • What evidence do we have that the supports provided are positively impacting, and supporting progress toward, the PLC+ initiative outcomes? • What additional supports are needed for the PLC+'s teacher-leaders to be fully successful in their roles?
6.3	The site or district leader(s) share PLC+ decision-making with the PLC+ members, offering them voice and choice in the operation of their PLC+.	• How do PLC+ members describe their interactions with site and/or district leader(s) specific to the PLC+ initiative? • What is the balance of PLC+-related decisions made among (a) PLC+ members only, (b) site or district leaders only, and (c) PLC+ members and site or district leaders together? • To what extent would PLC+ members agree that their voices and choices are honored by site and/or district leadership?
6.4	The shared and supportive leadership contributes to PLC+ members' feelings of efficacy within their schools.	• How do PLC+ members describe their efficacy within their schools? • How do PLC+ members describe the impact of the PLC+ initiative on their own perceived efficacy over time? • How do PLC+ members describe the impact of the PLC+ leadership on their own perceived efficacy over time?
6.5	The shared and supportive leadership contributes to measurably increased levels of trust between site or district leader(s) and PLC+ members.	• How do PLC+ members describe the level of trust between site and/or district leadership and the PLC+? • How has the level of trust between PLC+ members and site and/or district leadership changed over time? • Which specific and shared actions have increased, and which have reduced, trust between PLC+ members and site and/or district leadership?

online resources Available for download at **https://companion.corwin.com/courses/PLC**

CONCLUSION

PLC+ IS LIBERATORY

At its core, a PLC+ infused with Liberatory Design principles transforms collaboration from a routine practice into a revolutionary act of empowerment. As we have shown throughout this playbook, Liberatory Design, as outlined by the National Equity Project, invites educators to center the voices, experiences, and needs of students and communities. It challenges us to confront systemic inequities and co-create solutions that honor the humanity of every learner. A PLC+ rooted in these principles doesn't just focus on improving test scores or meeting accountability measures—it focuses on ensuring that every student thrives academically, socially, and emotionally in a system designed to support them.

Liberatory Design calls for educators to embrace inquiry with intentionality and humility. In a liberatory PLC+, the team asks not only "What is working?" but also "For whom is this working, and why?" This approach requires disrupting patterns of comfort, whether they appear in curriculum design, instructional strategies, or resource allocation. It also means making space for perspectives often excluded from decision-making, especially those of students and their families or guardians who experience barriers to access or success. Through protocols grounded in equity and fairness, a PLC+ teeam interrogates its own practices and biases, ensuring that their work does not perpetuate harm but instead cultivates belonging and possibility.

Liberatory PLC+ teams also prioritize action. Teams that reflect on gaps without taking steps to address them risk reinforcing those very gaps. The best solutions are co-created with a deep understanding of context and culture, centering on the lived realities of students. Whether the team and school are revising a unit plan to reflect student assets, redesigning assessments to be more inclusive of multilingual learners, or advocating for policy changes that address resource allocation, their work will thrive because it is deeply grounded in opportunities for all students to learn and grow. By taking courageous actions, teams turn their collective efficacy into a powerful force for transformation.

A liberatory PLC+ approach not only transforms student learning but also profoundly supports the growth and learning of teachers. By embedding Liberatory Design principles into the PLC+ process, educators are encouraged to adopt a mindset of continuous inquiry and reflection, which deepens their understanding of instructional practices as well as systemic barriers. Teachers learn to examine their own assumptions and practices, fostering greater self-awareness and professional growth. Collaborative work within this framework provides opportunities for collective problem-solving, shared ownership of challenges, and the co-creation of solutions that honor the diverse needs of all learners. This approach ensures that professional learning is dynamic, context-responsive, and empowering, allowing teachers to see themselves as agents of change. By addressing gaps and celebrating successes, PLC+ teams create a space where teachers feel supported, valued, and inspired to innovate, ensuring that their own professional learning aligns with the outcomes they strive to achieve for their students.

In this system, individual and collective efficacy are fostered. But even more than that, PLC+ is designed to create *collective effervescence,* a term coined by French sociologist Émile Durkheim more than a hundred years ago. Collective effervescence is "a state of intense shared emotional activation and sense of unison that emerges during instances of collective behavior."[105] It's that feeling of unity and connection that we crave. When powerful teams come together in a group focused on a shared purpose, there is a sense of energy and harmony, which contributes to our "internal barometer of well-being and perceived health."[106] Importantly, our teams and our students benefit when we find joy in our work and in our collaborations with others.

As this playbook comes to a close, the work of PLC+ teams is just beginning. It is an ongoing journey, not a destination. It demands that we embrace discomfort, navigate complexity, and remain steadfast in our commitment to learning. Liberatory Design provides the modes and mindset to meet this challenge, empowering educators to reimagine what is possible for their students, their schools, and their communities. In doing so, PLC+ becomes more than a professional learning structure—it becomes a movement where every student and educator can reach their fullest potential.

REFERENCES

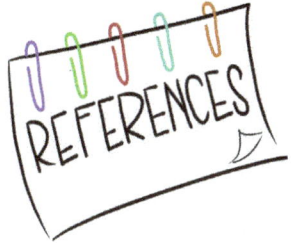

1. Vescio, V. i., Ross, D., & Adams, A. (2008). A review of research on the impact of professional learning communities on teaching practice and student learning. *Teaching and Teacher Education, 24*, 80–91.

2. Anaissie, T., Cary, V., Clifford, D., Malarkey, T., & Wise, S. (2021). *Liberatory Design: Mindsets and modes to design for equity*. http://www.liberatorydesign.com

3. Goddard, R., Hoy, W., & Hoy, A. (2000). Collective teacher efficacy: Its meaning, measure, and impact on student achievement. *American Educational Research Journal, 37*, 479–507.

4. Bandura, A. (1982). Self-efficacy mechanism in human agency. *American Psychologist, 37*, 122–147 (p. 143).

5. Sampson, R. J., Raudenbush, S. W., & Earls, F. (1997). Neighborhoods and violent crime: A multilevel study of collective efficacy. *Science, 277*(5328), 918–924.

6. Kim, M., & Shin, Y. (2015). Collective efficacy as a mediator between cooperative group norms and group positive affect and team creativity. *Asia Pacific Journal of Management, 32*(3), 693–716.

7. Hattie, J., Fisher, D., Frey, N., & Clarke, S. (2021). *Collective student efficacy: Developing independent and inter-dependent learners*. Corwin.

8. Vangrieken, K., Meredith, C., Packer, T., & Kyndt, E. (2017). Teacher communities as a context for professional development: A systematic review. *Teaching & Teacher Education, 61*, 47–59.

9. Lomos, C., Hofman, R. H., & Bosker, R. J. (2011). Professional communities and student achievement: A meta-analysis. *School Effectiveness & School Improvement, 22*(2), 121–148.

10. Bond, N. (2013). Developing a professional learning community among preservice teachers. *Current Issues in Education, 16*(2). http://cie.asu.edu/ojs/index.php/cieatasu/article/view/1053

11. Poortman, C. L., Brown, C., & Schildkamp, K. (2022). Professional learning networks: A conceptual model and research opportunities. *Educational Research, 64*(1), 95–112.

12. Brodie, K. (2021). Teacher agency in professional learning communities. *Professional Development in Education, 47*(4), 560–573.

13. OECD. (2021). *Positive, high-achieving students? What schools and teachers can do*. https://doi.org/10.1787/3b9551db-en

14. Tucker, M. (2017, September 6). Differences in performance WITHIN schools: Why so much greater than other countries? *Education Week*. https://www.edweek

15. Hord, S. M. (1980). *Working together: Cooperation or collaboration?* Research and Development Center for Teacher Education, University of Texas at Austin.

16. Faddis, T., Fisher, D., & Frey, N. (2022). *Collaborating though collective equity cycles: A playbook for ensuring all students and teachers succeed.* Corwin.

17. Fisher, D., Frey, N., Almarode, J., Flories, K., & Nagel, D. (2019). *PLC+: Better decisions and greater impact by design.* Corwin.

18. Barnatt, J., Gahlsdorf Terrell, D., D'Souza, L. A., Jong, C., Cochran-Smith, M., Viesca, K. M., Gleeson, A. M., McQuillan, P., & Shakman, K. (2017). Interpreting early career trajectories. *Educational Policy, 31*(7), 992–1032.

19. Brunner, M., Keller, U., Wenger, M., Fischbach, A., & Lüdtke, O. (2018). Between-school variation in students' achievement, motivation, affect, and learning strategies: Results from 81 countries for planning group-randomized trials in education. *Journal of Research on Educational Effectiveness, 11*(3), 452–478.

20. Yeager, D. (2024). *10 to 25: The science of motivating young people.* Simon & Schuster.

21. Eells, R. (2011). *Meta-analysis of the relationship between collective efficacy and student achievement.* Unpublished doctoral dissertation. Loyola University of Chicago.

22. Anaissie, T., Cary, V., Clifford, D., Malarkey, T., & Wise, S. (2021). *Liberatory Design: Mindsets and modes to design for equity.* http://www.liberatorydesign.com

23. National Equity Project (2024). Leading for Equity Framework. https://www.nationalequityproject.org/framework/leading-for-equity-framework

24. Anaissie, T., Cary, V., Clifford, D., Malarkey, T., & Wise, S. (2021). Liberatory Design: Mindsets and modes to design for equity. http://www.liberatorydesign.com *Attribution-NonCommercial-ShareAlike* 3.0 Unported (CC BY-NC-SA 3.0).

25. Deming, E. (2000). *Out of the crisis.* MIT Press.

26. TNTP. (2024). *The opportunity makers: How a diverse group of public schools helps students catch-up and how far more can.* https://tntp.org/wp-content/uploads/2024/09/The-Opportunity-Makers-TNTP.pdf

27. Almarode, J., Frey, N., Fisher, D., & Barbee, K. (2025). *Teacher clarity.* Corwin.

28. Rubie-Davies, C. (2014). *Becoming a high expectation teacher: Raising the bar.* Routledge.

29. Steiner, D. (2024). The unrealized promise of high-quality instructional materials. *State Education Standard, 24*(1). https://www.nasbe.org/the-unrealized-promise-of-high-quality-instructional-materials/

30. Gorman, N. (2017, February 7). Survey finds teachers spend 7 hours per week searching for instructional materials. *Education World.* https://www.educationworld.com/a_news/survey-finds-teachers-spend-7-hours-week-searching-instructional-materials-490526015

31. Steiner, D. (2024). The unrealized promise of high-quality instructional materials. *State Education Standard, 24*(1). https://www.nasbe.org/the-unrealized-promise-of-high-quality-instructional-materials/

32. Fisher, D., Frey, N., Almarode, J., Barbee, K., Amador, O., & Assof, J. (2024). *The teacher clarity playbook: A hands-on guide to creating learning intentions and success criteria for organized, effective instruction* (2nd ed.). Corwin.

33. Serki, N., & Bolkan, S. (2023). The effect of clarity on learning: Impacting motivation through cognitive load. *Communication Education, 73*(1), 29–45. https://doi.org/10.1080/03634523.2023.2250883

34. Verso Learning. (2021). https://www.versolearning.com

35. Lassiter, C., Fisher, D., Frey, N., & Smith, D. (2022). *How leadership works: A playbook for instructional leaders*. Corwin.

36. Lassiter, C., Fisher, D., Frey, N., & Smith, D. (2022). *How leadership works: A playbook for instructional leaders*. Corwin.

37. Guskey, T. R. (2005). Mapping the road to proficiency. *Educational Leadership, 63*(3), 32–38.

38. Wattenberg, R. (2024). How background knowledge builds good readers and why knowledge building ELA curricula are vital. *State Education Standard, 24*(1). https://www.nasbe.org/how-background-knowledge-builds-good-readers-and-why-knowledge-building-ela-curricula-are-vital/

38. Ausubel, D. P. (1968). *Educational psychology: A cognitive view* (p. vi). Holt, Rinehart and Winston.

40. Nuthall, G. A. (2007). *The hidden lives of learners*. New Zealand Council for Educational Research.

41. Koedinger, K. R., Carvalho, P. F., Liu, R., & McLaughlin, E. A. (2023). An astonishing regularity in student learning rate. *Proceedings of the National Academy of Sciences, 120*(13), Article e2221311120.

42. Valencia, R. R. (2010). *Dismantling contemporary deficit thinking: Educational thought and practice*. Routledge.

43. Grant, A. (2023). *Hidden potential: The science of achieving greater things* (p. 206). Viking.

44. Ainsworth, L. (2013). *Prioritizing the Common Core: Identifying specific standards to emphasize the most* (p. vx). Corwin.

45. Kramer, S. (2015). *How to leverage PLCs for school improvement*. Solution Tree. https://cloudfront-s3.solutiontree.com/pdfs/Reproducibles_HLPLCSI/essentialstandardscriteria.pdf

46. Kramer, S. (2015). *How to leverage PLCs for school improvement*. Solution Tree. https://cloudfront-s3.solutiontree.com/pdfs/Reproducibles_HLPLCSI/essentialstandardscriteria.pdf

47. Fullan, M., & Quinn, J. (2015). *Coherence: The right drivers in action for schools, districts, and systems*. Corwin.

48. Lindvall, J., & Ryve, A. (2019). Coherence and the positioning of teachers in professional development programs. A systematic review. *Educational Research Review, 27*, 140–154.

49. Knasel, E., Meed, J., Rossetti, A., Read, H., & Record, D. (2006). *Improving initial assessment: Guide to good practice*. https://files.eric.ed.gov/fulltext/ED498597.pdf

50. https://www.slu.edu/cttl/resources/resource-guides/strengths-based-education.pdf

51. National Equity Project. (2015). *Equity-centered professional learning communities.*

52. National Equity Project. (2015). *Equity-centered professional learning communities.*

53. Anaissie, T., Cary, V., Clifford, D., Malarkey, T., & Wise, S. (2021). *Liberatory Design: Mindsets and modes to design for equity.* http://www.liberatorydesign.com.

54. National Equity Project. (nd). Learning Partnerships. https://www.nationalequityproject.org/frameworks/learning-partnerships

55. Anaissie, T., Cary, V., Clifford, D., Malarkey, T., & Wise, S. (2021). *Liberatory Design: Mindsets and modes to design for equity.* http://www.liberatorydesign.com

56. National Equity Project (nd). Why Focal Students. nationalequityproject.org/frameworks/focal-students

57. Anaissie, T., Cary, V., Clifford, D., Malarkey, T., & Wise, S. (2021). *Liberatory Design: Mindsets and modes to design for equity.* http://www.liberatorydesign.com

58. Frey, N., Fisher, D., & Hattie, J. (2017). Surface, deep, and transfer? Considering the role of content literacy instructional strategies. *Journal of Adolescent & Adult Literacy, 60*(5), 567–575.

59. Garrett, R., & Hong, G. (2016). Impacts of grouping and time on the math learning of language minority kindergartners. *Educational Evaluation & Policy Analysis, 38*(2), 222–244.

60. TNTP & ReadWorks. (2022). *Unlocking acceleration: How below-grade level work is holding students back in literacy.* https://tntp.org/assets/documents/Unlocking_Acceleration_8.16.22.pdf

61. Rosenshine, B. (2012). Principles of instruction: Research-based strategies that all teachers should know. *American Educator, 36*(1), 12–39. https:// www.visiblelearningmetax.com

62. Hattie, J. A., & Donoghue, G. M. (2016). Learning strategies: A synthesis and conceptual model. *Nature/NPJ: Science of Learning.* https://doi.org/10.1038/npjscilearn.2016.13

63. Ruiz-Martín, H., & Bybee, R. W. (2002). The cognitive principles of learning underlying the 5E Model of Instruction. *International Journal of STEM Education,* Article 9, 21. https://doi.org/10.1186/s40594-022-00337-z

64. Hunter, M. (1982). *Mastery teaching.* Corwin.

65. Fisher, D., & Frey, N. (2021). *Better learning through structured teaching: A framework for the gradual release of responsibility* (3rd ed.). ASCD.

66. Education Trust. (2015). *Checking in: Do classroom assignments reflect today's higher standards?*

67. Education Trust. (2018). *Checking in: Are math assignments measuring up?*

68. Rubie-Davies, C. M. (2015). *Becoming a high expectation teacher: Raising the bar.* Taylor & Francis.

69. Rubie-Davies, C. M., Peterson, E. R., Sibley, C. G., & Rosenthal, R. (2015). A teacher expectation intervention: Modelling the practices of high expectation teachers. *Contemporary Educational Psychology, 40,* 72–85.

70. Linchevski, L., & Kutscher, B. (1998). Tell me with whom you're learning, and I'll tell you how much you've learned: Mixed ability versus same-ability grouping in mathematics. *Journal for Research in Mathematics Education, 29,* 533–554.

71. Pfleging, A., & Cunningham, K. E. (2021). Efficacy in the face of adversity. *Educational Leadership, 79*(3), 70–75.

72. Campbell, V. A., Antony, M., Zulawski, J., & Foley, K. (2024). The effects of attending high individual and collective teacher efficacy schools on ninth grade on-track. *Education Sciences, 14*(5), 546. https://doi.org/10.3390/educsci14050546

73. Campbell, V. A., Antony, M., Zulawski, J., & Foley, K. (2024). The effects of attending high individual and collective teacher efficacy schools on ninth grade on-track. *Education Sciences, 14*(5), 546. https://doi.org/10.3390/educsci14050546

74. Fink, D. (Ed.). (2016). *Trust and verify: The real keys to school improvement.* University College London Institute of Education Press.

75. Ford, T. G. (2019). Can the use of informal control mechanisms increase trust among teachers? An evaluation of the Accelerated Schools intervention. *Studies in Educational Evaluation, 63,* 59–71.

76. Tschannen-Moran, M. (2001). The effects of a state-wide conflict management initiative in schools. *American Secondary Education, 29*(3), 2–32.

77. Evans, M., Teasdale, R., Gannon-Slater, N., La Londe, P., Crenshaw, H., Greene, J., & Schwandt, T. (2019). "How did that happen?" Teachers' explanations for low test scores. *Teachers College Record, 121*(2), 1–40.

78. Ford, T. G. (2019). Can the use of informal control mechanisms increase trust among teachers? An evaluation of the Accelerated Schools intervention. *Studies in Educational Evaluation, 63,* 59–71.

79. Wiliam, D., Fisher, D., & Frey, N. (2024). *Student assessment: Better evidence, better decisions, better learning.* Corwin.

80. Wiliam, D., Fisher, D., & Frey, N. (2024). *Student assessment: Better evidence, better decisions, better learning.* Corwin.

81. Ribosa, J., Corcelles, S. M., Morodo, A., & Duran, D. (2024). Reducing teachers' resistance to reciprocal peer observation. *European Journal of Education, 59*(2), 1–21.

82. Miranda, J. P., Batista, M., Duarte, C., & Sanches, T. (2021). Interdisciplinary class observation in higher education: Lessons learned from the professional development experience of four teachers. *Education Sciences, 11*(11), 706. https://doi.org/10.3390/educsci11110706

83. Ross, P., & Gibson, S. A. (2010). Exploring a conceptual framework for expert noticing during literacy instruction. *Literacy Research and Instruction, 49*(2), 175–193.

84. Allen, D. W. (1966). A new framework for in-service education. *High School Journal, 49*(8), 355–362.

85. Fisher, D., & Frey, N. (2014). Using teacher learning walks to improve instruction. *Principal Leadership, 14*(5), 58–61.

86. City, E. A., Elmore, R. F., Fiarman, S. E., & Teitel, L. (2009). *Instructional rounds in education.* Harvard Education Press.

87. Anaissie, T., Cary, V., Clifford, D., Malarkey, T., & Wise, S. (2021). *Liberatory Design: Mindsets and modes to design for equity.* http://www.liberatorydesign.com

88. National Equity Project. (2015). *Equity-centered professional learning communities.*

89. Student Achievement Partners. (n.d.). *Juicy sentence guidance*. https://achievethecore.org/content/upload/Juicy%20Sentence%20Guidance.pdf

90. Anaissie, T., Cary, V., Clifford, D., Malarkey, T., & Wise, S. (2021). *Liberatory Design: Mindsets and modes to design for equity*. http://www.liberatorydesign.com

91. Castillo, J. M., Scheel, N. L., Wolgemuth, J. R., Latimer, J. D., & Green, S. M. (2022). A scoping review of the literature on professional learning for MTSS. *Journal of School Psychology, 92*, 166–187.

92. Datnow, A., & Park, V. (2018). Opening or closing doors for students? Equity and data use in schools. *Journal of Educational Change, 19*(2), 131–152.

93. Schildkamp, K., & Datnow, A. (2022). When data teams struggle: Learning from less successful data use efforts. *Leadership & Policy in Schools, 21*(2), 147–166.

94. Senge, P. M. (2012). *Schools that learn: A fifth discipline fieldbook for educators, parents, and everyone who cares about education* (2nd ed.). Nicholas Brealey.

95. Chew, S. L., & Cerbin, W. J. (2020). The cognitive challenges of effective teaching. *Journal of Economic Education, 52*(1), 17–40.

96. Anaissie, T., Cary, V., Clifford, D., Malarkey, T., & Wise, S. (2021). *Liberatory Design: Mindsets and modes to design for equity*. http://www.liberatorydesign.com

97. Senge, P. M. (2012). *Schools that learn: A fifth discipline fieldbook for educators, parents, and everyone who cares about education (2nd ed.)*. Nicholas Brealey.

98. Boughzala, I., & de Vreede, G. J. (2015). Evaluating team collaboration quality: The development and field application of a collaboration maturity model. *Journal of Management Information Systems, 32*(3), 129–157. https://doi.org/10.1080/07421222.2015.1095042

99. Powell, J. (nd). On belonging. Retrieved from https://neighborhoodbirthcenter.org/blog-1/2019/3/5/blog-2

100. Hirsch, S. (2010). Collective responsibility makes all teachers the best. *Teachers Teaching Teachers*. https://learningforward.org/docs/leading-teacher/sept10_hirsh.pdf?sfvrsn=2

101. Frey, N., Nagel, D., Fisher, D., Faddis, T., & Allen-Rotell, A. (2024). *PLC+: A playbook for instructional leaders*. Corwin.

102. Hattie, J., Fisher, D., Frey, N., & Almarode, J. (2024). *The illustrated guide to visible learning: An introduction to what works best in schools*. Corwin.

103. Carter, E. W. (2021). Dimensions of belonging for individuals with intellectual and developmental disabilities. In J. L. Jones & K. L. Gallus (Eds.), *Belonging and resilience in individuals with developmental disabilities* (pp. 13–33). Springer Nature.

104. Lassiter, C., Fisher, D., Faddis, T., & Frey, N. (2024). *How teams work: A playbook for distributing leadership*. Corwin.

105. Pizarro, J. J., Zumeta, L. N., Bouchat, P., Włodarczyk, A., Rimé, B., Basabe, N., Amutio, A., & Páez, D. (2022). Emotional processes, collective behavior, and social movements: A meta-analytic review of collective effervescence outcomes during collective gatherings and demonstrations. *Frontiers in Psychology, 13*: Article 974683. https//doi.org/10.3389/fpsyg.2022.974683.

106. Malchiodi, C. (2021, August 1). Please don't take my collective effervescence away. *Psychology Today*. https://www.psychologytoday.com/us/blog/arts-and-health/202108/please-don-t-take-my-collective-effervescence-away

INDEX

Academic standards
   analysis, 51, 54–56, 55–56 (figure), 58, 78, 111
   table of specifications, 65, 65–66 (figure)
   teacher clarity protocol, 62–63
Acceleration, 103, 126
Activators, 25, 44, 70, 126, 134, 192
Almarode, J., 75
Assessment functions, 138
   decision-driven data collection, 138–139
   formative assessment practices, 139
   phrases, 138
   students' learning, 138
Assignment analysis tools, 111
Ausubel, D. P., 75

Capacity-building learning, 152–154
Carter, E. W., 201
Chatbot, 61, 67, 86, 119, 140, 172, 173, 185
Cognitive barriers, 179–181, 179–181 (figure)
Collaborative teams, 17, 205
Collective efficacy, 2, 4, 7, 21, 24, 160, 187, 230
   attributes, 7–8
   collaboration and, 197
   equity and, 156
   individual and, 25, 44, 70, 96, 126, 192
   within PLCs, 204
   student achievement, 200
   teachers, 7, 133, 153
Collective learning, intentional domain, 217–221
Collective responsibility, 7, 136, 199, 203
Collegial processes domain, 209–212
Common challenge, 40–41, 188–189
   data analyzing, 187
   debriefing protocol, 182
   liberatory design modes, 42
   post-investigation protocol, 188–189
Cooperative teams, 17
Critical dialogue, 134–136

Crosscutting values
   activators, 25
   consistency status, 126
   educational experiences, 96
   equity and fairness, 24–25
   expectations, high, 25
   grade-level standards, 70
   individual and collective efficacy, 25
   professional learning community status, 44
   progress and achievement, 192
   team prototype, 160

Data analysis, 20, 92, 93, 189
Data-informed decisions, 21
Deep-learning instructional strategies, 108, 108 (figure)
Deming, E., 42

The Education Trust, 111, 119–120
Educators, 4, 7, 20, 111, 179
   collective efficacy, 25
   evidence-based framework, 107
   iterative process, 11
   PLC+ model, 21
   skills and effectiveness, 10, 54
   students' interactions, 123
   See also Liberatory Design approaches
Empathy mapping, 30, 37–39, 187
End-of-unit assessments, 170, 171–172 (figure)
Endurance, 79
Equity and fairness, 4, 24, 29, 44, 70, 96, 156, 160, 192, 229
Evidence-based instructional strategies, 20, 52, 102, 104, 105, 107, 127, 157
   deep-learning, 108, 108 (figure)
   identification, 157
   mega meta-analyses, 107
   student achievement, 107
   surface-level, 107–108, 108 (figure)
   transfer learning, 109, 109 (figure)

Fairness. *See* Equity and fairness
Firm foundation domain, 205–208
Focal students, 88–90, 90 (figure)
    achievement/progress map, 180, 180–181 (figure)
    checking in, 183–185, 184–185 (figure)
    classroom improvements, 185
    individual engagement, 183
    instructional strategies, 156
    interview questions, 183–184, 184–185 (figure)
    learning from, 156–157
    PLC+ team, 88, 157
Ford, T. G., 133, 135
Formative assessment cycles, 139, 139 (figure)
    long-cycle, 139
    medium-cycle, 139
    short-cycle, 139

Grade-level expectations, 79
Grant, A., 78
Green Valley Elementary School, 69

Hattie, J., 107
Heterogeneous grouping of students, 122–123
High-expectation teachers (HET), 122
High-quality instructional materials (HQIMs), 52, 111
Hindered communication, 133
Hord, S. M., 17, 205

Individual efficacy, 7, 25, 44, 70, 96, 126, 192
    See also Collective efficacy
Initial assessments, effective, 81–82
Instructional factors, 179–181, 179–181 (figure)
Instructional time, 65, 77
Investigation cycle, 19–20, 105, 187
    PLC+ team, 88
    statements, 33
    trial and refinement, 16

Kramer, S., 79

Leadership, shared and supportive domain, 225–228
Learning intentions, 58, 120, 193
    and success criteria, 20, 60, 63–64
    teacher clarity protocol, 63
    See also Success criteria
Liberatory Design approaches, 2, 3, 24, 131, 165
    authentic engagement, 29
    BIPOC teachers, 29
    challenges identification, 33
    common challenge protocol, 40–41
    decision-making, 29–30
    educators, 37
    mindset, 183
    PLC+ participants, 33, 168
    principles, 183, 229–230
    steps, 30
Lincoln Middle School, 125
Literacy assignment analysis tool, 112–114
Low-expectation teachers (LET), 122

Mathematics assignments analysis tool, 115–119
Microteaching
    feedback, 147
    protocol, 148–150

National Equity Project (NEP), 2, 28, 88, 204, 229
North Central High School, 95

One-dimensional evidence model, 174

Peers supporting peers, 221–224
Performance assessments, 170, 171–172 (figure)
Performance map, 176
    individual and environmental factors, 177
    professional learning community, 176
    trends and patterns, 176, 176 (figure)
Phases of learning, 103
PLC+ framework, 2, 66, 197–200
    design features, 3–5
    guiding questions, 5–6
    investigation cycles, 19–21
    Liberatory Design, 27–30

    needs assessment scale, 206, 210,
        214, 218, 222, 226
    progress assessment scale, 207–208,
        211, 219, 223, 227
    readiness assessment tool, 205
    success planning, 200–201,
        201–202 (figure)
    team's assessment, 212, 216,
        220, 224, 228
PLC+ teams, 2, 6, 24, 101, 111, 138, 205, 230
    chatbot, 67
    common challenge, 33
    learning partnerships, 88
    microteaching, 147, 149–150
    See-Engage-Act heuristics, 166
    self-awareness, 28–29
    situational awareness, 29
    team meetings, 90
Private practice, 159
Professional learning community
    (PLC), 1, 38, 101, 152, 176
    accountability and collaboration, 10, 11
    clarity and shared purpose, 16
    collaboration time and structure, 17
    collective efficacy, 7–8
    common challenges, 33–34
    complementary purposes, 10
    conventional practices, 15
    cooperation and collaboration, 17
    design feature, two truths and a lie, 9
    essential question, 8
    investigation cycles, 11–12
Programme for International
    Student Assessment (PISA), 133
Protocols
    capacity-building learning
        walk, 153–154
    common challenge, 40–42
    data analysis, 92–93
    description, 3
    mathematics assignment
        analysis tool, 115–119
    microteaching, 149–150
    post-investigation common
        challenge, 188–189
    reciprocal peer observation, 143–145
    teacher clarity, 63–64

QR codes, 8, 12, 39, 41, 43, 49,
    79, 102, 114, 132, 159, 175, 202

Readiness Assessment Tool, 79, 205
    firm foundation, 205–208
    intentional collective learning,
        217–221
    peers supporting peers, 221–224
    shared and supportive
        leadership, 225–228
    shared vision and values, 213–216
    supportive relationships, 209–212
Reciprocal peer observations, 142–145
Risk-taking, innovation and, 44,
    133, 135–136, 230
Rubie-Davies, C., 122

See-Engage-Act heuristics,
    design inquiry, 166
Self-assessment, 45–46, 71, 97, 127, 161
Self-awareness, 28–29
Self-efficacy, 122, 133
Self-reflection, 203
Senge, P. M., 168, 187
Shared experiences, 134–135
Situational awareness, 28–29
SMART goals, 33
Standards, analyzing. *See*
    Academic standards
Stanford Teacher Preparation
    Program, 147
State Board of Education, California, 50
Strengths-based approach,
    77, 84–85 (figure)
    educational supports, 84
    grade-level expectations, 79
    "if/then" statements, 85–86
    math assessment, 86, 86 (figure)
    mindset, 78, 85
    selection criteria, 78–79
    "Where are we now?", 78
Student-centered analysis, 20, 33, 37
Student learning, 1, 5, 8, 10, 16,
    21, 33, 42, 105, 134
    acceleration and remediation, 103
    and achievement, 9
    biases, 97
    confirmative assessment, 65
    data and student work, 20
    goals setting, 25
    learning community, 134
    PLC+ approach, 230
    proficiency, 79

teaching practices, 11
team members, 199
Success criteria, 60, 61, 64, 71
  assessment opportunities, 149
  building, 205
  development, 63
  expectations, high, 81
  learning progressions, 193
  monitoring, 203–204, 204 (figure)
  planning, 200–201, 201–202 (figure)
  self-reflection, 203
  for students, 20
  See also Learning intentions

Supportive relationships domain, 209–212
Surface-level instructional strategies, 107–108, 108 (figure), 140

Table of specifications, 65, 66 (figure)
Teacher clarity protocol, 20, 50, 63–64
Teacher teams, 49
Transfer learning instructional strategies, 109, 109 (figure)
Tucker, M., 16

The Visible Learning Progress, 107, 175

CORWIN

To help every educator help every student

We believe that every single student deserves a great education

We believe that knowing our impact is both a privilege and a responsibility

We believe that a fair, stable, and thriving society is built on education

Take your teaching further

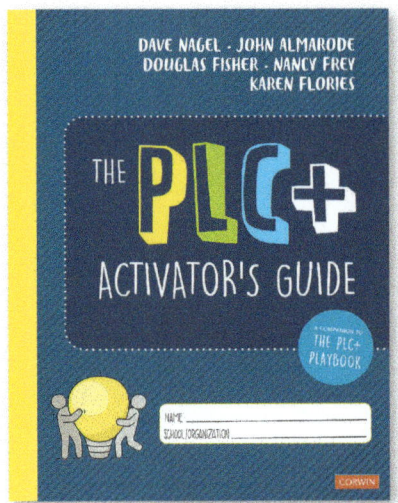
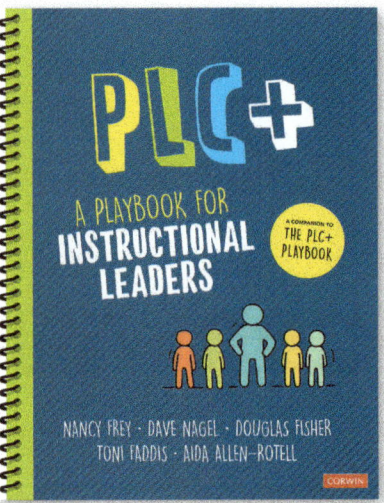
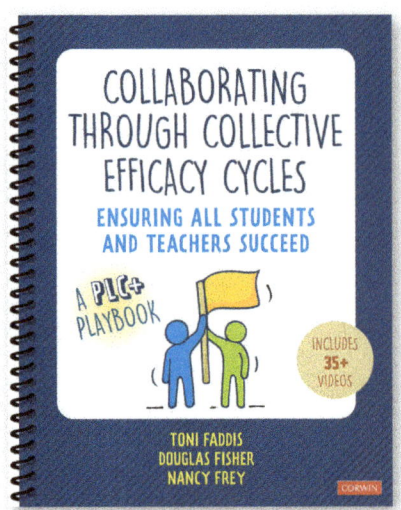
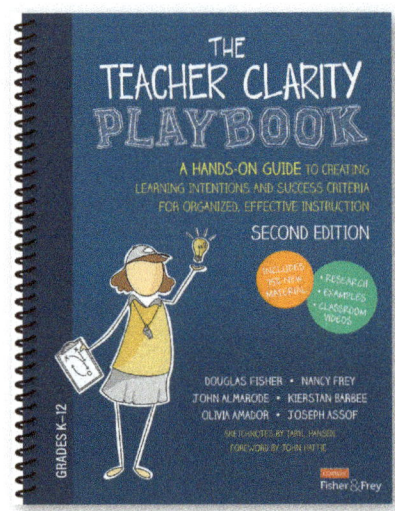
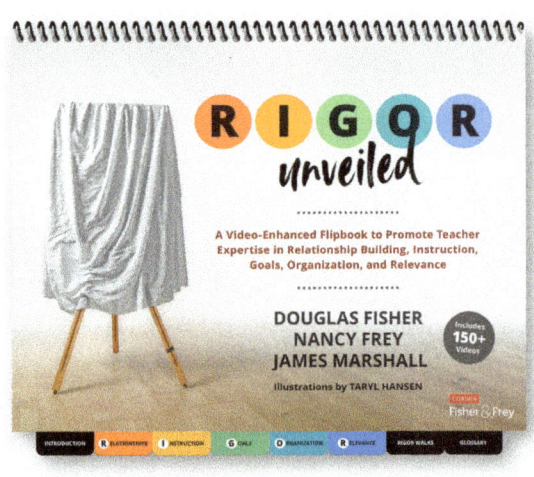

You may also be interested in...

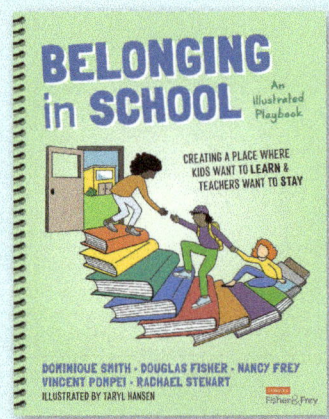

To learn more, visit corwin.com

Put your learning into practice

When you're ready to take your learning deeper, begin your journey with our PD services. Our personalized professional learning workshops are designed for schools or districts who want to engage in high-quality PD with a certified consultant, measure their progress, and evaluate their impact on student learning.

CORWIN PLC+

Empower teacher teams to build collective agency and remove learning barriers

It's not enough to just build teacher agency, we must also focus on the power of the collective. Empowering your PLCs is a step toward becoming better equipped educators with greater credibility to foster successful learners.

Get started at corwin.com/plc

CORWIN Teacher Clarity

Students learn more when expectations are clear

As both a method and a mindset, Teacher Clarity allows the classroom to transform into a place where teaching is made clear. Learn how to explicitly communicate to students what they will be learning on a given day, why they're learning it, and how to know if they were successful.

Get started at corwin.com/teacherclarity

CORWIN Visible Learning

Translate the science of how we learn into practices for the classroom

Discover how learning works and how this translates into potential for enhancing and accelerating learning. Learn how to develop a shared language of learning and implement the science of learning in schools and classrooms.

Get started at corwin.com/visiblelearning

Experience the Corwin Difference.
Learn more at corwin.com/the-corwin-difference

CORWIN